Praise for Sean Senechal and her work:

"Sean Senechal redefines the concept of language . . . in this novel and exciting approach with immense perspectives and potentially dramatic consequences for our understanding of communication. . . . In the last decades, our relation to companion animals has taken new dimensions. . . . Maybe we are now on the verge of another big leap where communication between different species takes a huge step forward."
>—Roger Abrantes, Ph.D., author of *Dog Language*

"AnimalSign is a powerful approach enhancing companion animals' abilities to communicate with us. Ms. Senechal regards her human and animal students as productive language learners. This opens up an exciting new path for interspecies communication and studies!"
>—Penny Patterson, Ph.D., The Gorilla Foundation Koko.org

"I asked Sean Senechal to teach my horse simple EquineSigns. One day, my horse used those 'signs' to call my attention to her little friend, whose neck was dangerously caught in a fence. By communicating we, together, saved her friend's life."
>—Laura Pasten, DVM, author of *How Smart Is Your Puppy?*

"I've just finished reading your fantastic book, and I'm thrilled to begin working with my dogs! I'm also very impressed by the knowledge that you have and by the techniques in animal language that you have invented. Your animal communication approach . . . is simply a revolution!"
>—Danielle Gauthier de Varennes, editor of Canada's *Canis Familiaris*

Dogs Can Sign, Too

A Breakthrough Method for Teaching Your Dog to Communicate to You

SEAN SENECHAL

CELESTIAL ARTS
Berkeley

Copyright © 2009 by Sean Senechal
Photographs copyright © 2009 by Drew Parsons
The photographs on pages 134, 136, 172, 175, 184, and 190, copyright © 2009 by Sean C. Senechal
The photograph on page 126, copyright © 2009 by ShutterStock Images
The photograph on page 196, copyright © 2009 by Michele Crompton
Front cover photo, top, and back cover photos copyright © 2009 by Drew Parsons
Front cover photos, bottom, copyright © 2009 by ShutterStock Images

All rights reserved.
Published in the United States by Celestial Arts, an imprint of the
Crown Publishing Group, a division of Random House, Inc., New York
www.crownpublishing.com
www.tenspeed.com

Celestial Arts and the Celestial Arts colophon are registered trademarks of Random House, Inc.

AnimalSign®, ASL® (as in K9*ASL* and Equine*ASL*, K9Sign™, and EquineSign™, are registered trademarks or trademarks of Sean C. Senechal.

Frisbee® is a registered trademark of Wham-O, Inc. All rights reserved.

Library of Congress Cataloging-in-Publication Data

Senechal, Sean.
  Dogs can sign, too : a breakthrough method for teaching your dog to communicate to you / Sean Senechal.
      p. cm.
  Includes bibliographical references and index.
  ISBN-13: 978-1-58761-353-1 (alk. paper)
  ISBN-10: 1-58761-353-0 (alk. paper)
  1. Dogs—Training. 2. Sign language. 3. Human-animal communication.
I. Title.

  SF431.S42 2009
  636.7'0887—dc22

2009012052
ISBN 978-1-58761-353-1

Printed in the United States of America

Cover and text design by Katy Brown

10 9 8 7 6 5 4 3 2 1

First Edition

TO ANGELFUR

Watching us sign for years, she finally joined the conversation.

Contents

Imagine! Your dog Jazz runs up to the bathroom, where you are in the shower. Jazz barks, you say, "Just a minute." The barks become frantic, so you peer out of the shower to see Jazz signing *Mary, Down, Breath Not, Basement.* You jump out of the shower, run to the basement to find Mary on the floor and not breathing. You perform CPR and as she gasps, you realize that without Jazz signing the details, you wouldn't have responded so fast, and Mary may not have survived.

Imagine! Your dog Peaches looks a bit distressed. You K9Sign *What?* She signs *Sharp* and shows you her paw. You inspect her paw but can't find anything. You sign *Which?* then sign *Sharp* with your left hand and sign *Dull* with your right. She taps your left hand meaning *Sharp.* You inspect between her pads with a magnifier and see redness and a very small piece of glass, which you remove. You ask *Where's Glass?* Peaches signs *Room 5, Under Table.* You go to room 5 (the bathroom) and sweep up the remaining glass on the floor under the table.

Introduction

AnimalSign Language is a revolutionary approach to human-animal communication. This made-for, animal-friendly sign language is designed to provide nonprimate animals with their own expanded, gestural language so that they can sign to us. With this new perspective toward animal communication, imagine the linguistic frontier that we will open up for animals who are capable of learning both receptive and productive language. Imagine literate canines who can finally answer your question, "Why are you barking?" Imagine what they might be able to communicate.

Animals use their own natural, body gestures (including vocalizations) to communicate. AnimalSign Language extends beyond these natural gestures into the realm of learned language. Gestures and signs have been taught to primates, such as gorillas, chimpanzees, bonobos, and of course, humans. We humans have many languages to choose from. Now, with AnimalSign, in particular K9Sign, nonprimates can learn to sign to us, not just understand what we sign to them.

AnimalSign Language for dogs is called K9Sign Language. In this book, you will learn the language, background, and practical art of teaching K9Sign Language to humans and dogs. Anything a dog can identify can be linked to a word and a corresponding body gesture. Those learned, organized body gestures can make up a language. With this language, dogs will have the expanded tools to communicate to you. Most of the words that make up this learned language are not in the natural body language that has been extensively documented in dogs. K9Sign Language needs to be taught. The language lessons in chapters 8 and 9 are presented with the expectation that your student will:

- learn the gestures as signs, as representations of objects/events,
- make up new gestures,
- combine gestures,
- communicate details of its concerns,
- be understood.

Whether dogs use the lessons for tricks or for simple or complex communications, the benefits to animals and humans are worth the effort. The organization of animal gestures into a structured, standardized language profoundly expands the potential for human-animal communication, bonding, fulfillment, and scientific understanding.

K9Sign Language views dogs as *receptive* and *productive* language learners. Receptive language refers to understanding language. For example, a dog can understand and act on the communication ***Bring Ball.*** Productive language refers to expressing language, such as vocalizing or gesturing to communicate, as in barking, or signing ***I'll Get Ball.*** Though some animals currently learn language receptively, and have some natural productive language, I believe those skills are an underachievement. Dogs have the potential to do more.

Dogs are already somewhat literate. They learn to understand aspects of our many languages (vocal and gestural); they learn to understand their own species' natural communications. But, in comparison to their language potential, they are currently illiterate. I believe their productive literacy might be similar to that of very young human children. They might have ideas to express but do not yet have the (agreed-upon) vocabulary to express details. Language education may not only increase their vocabulary, but also their brain development, helping them to sharpen their thoughts as well.

Animals can produce language (beyond the natural) if we invest in them. We simply need to teach them as we do our children—in small steps, with patience and repetition.

Language learning takes time. Some excited teachers expect animals to learn K9Sign in a month, though humans take years to fully learn a language. Teaching K9Sign involves the use of existing and new training (education) approaches to weave meaning into the learned moves, or gestures. The gesture-moves and their meanings are logically organized into a structured language, K9Sign. With a language to use, animal literacy is imaginable.

What do animal enthusiasts think about AnimalSign? Those I pose the question to generally respond that we all sign in one way or another to our animals. After I explain that AnimalSign Language is about animals signing *to* us, people say, "Ohhh! Tell me about it. How do you do this? How can I use it?" Most people seem delighted with the idea of animal language and literacy. To those who say this is an impossibility, I say let the animals tell us! Someday I will ask my animals, ***What Do You Think About Signing?*** My horse Princess will surely sign, ***More, More.*** My dog Chal will give it a paws-up! After reading this book, I expect you'll give it a thumbs-up!

My vision for K9Sign Language is for dogs to use learned gestures to communicate in greater detail than what we have observed from their natural canine body gestures, and for humans to open up to the possibility that animals can learn to sign in meaningful ways that suggest true language.

The goals of an AnimalSign Language education are to provide animals with the skills to communicate their perceptions and desires, for humans to better understand (nonprimate) animal cognition, and to enrich—experientially and functionally—our human-animal relationships. For animals and the general public, communicating through AnimalSign has the great potential to be both useful and fulfilling. In the hands of creative researchers and teacher-trainers, the language development findings and uses are endless. As we communicate with AnimalSigns, gathering data and evidence of its effectiveness (supportive or not), we can determine its status as a language. Is a dog using K9Sign as true language, as communication, or as she might perform a trick? Keep an open mind. First teach your dog to sign, then you will have the experience to answer this question.

Once Upon a Dream

At the workshops and events I teach or attend, people often ask how I conceived the idea for AnimalSign and created the language. They are curious to know if teaching animals to communicate through signs began as a scientific or personal endeavor. The answer is both. It began as a personal quest and later evolved into a scientific one. While at graduate school, I experienced months of intense dreams revolving around horses. What was it about these horses that affected me so deeply? Consciously horses represented a drive for noble causes, truth, integrity, beauty, and deep feeling. I had ridden a horse only once. Why were they in my dreams? I set out on an exploration to find out. Walking through several barns, I stood in front of each horse, but none personally engaged me, nor I them. When I arrived at the Stanford Red Barn in Palo Alto, I heard someone say a yearling was in the back stall. I walked toward the stall and peeked over the door. There she was, Princess, looking right at me with an intense, electrifying expression. She was a dark, shiny, Dutch Warmblood/Thoroughbred mix. I was awestruck. She was beautiful and so communicative. Bonded, I had to know her.

Having studied primate learning and human attention at UC Davis's animal physiology graduate school, combined with my previous experience with dogs, I was able to teach Princess moves, tricks, then gestures, and signs for us to communicate. She would mix and match her gestures, some natural, some learned, most often "saying" things I didn't understand at first. But she initiated and enjoyed communicating using her natural and the newly learned gestures I had taught her. She engaged and inspired me to interact and communicate with her.

Teaching an animal a sign language had already been accomplished at various levels by Beatrice and Alan Gardner (with the now famous chimpanzee Washoe) and by Francine "Penny" Patterson with Koko, a gorilla. Penny and Koko even lived nearby. Knowing someone had successfully found a way to communicate with an animal encouraged me whenever I felt stuck. At one point, I even contacted Dr. Penny Patterson and she kindly visited us, bringing along a knowledgeable horse friend. Dr. Patterson, though keeping her distance, was very perceptive and observant, often asking about a gesture's meaning I had not noticed.

Over time AnimalSign and EquineSign evolved, and I found a Monterey County ranch suitable for Princess and me to live and work together. While earning a teaching credential, I integrated what I was learning about teaching humans with what I already knew about teaching Princess. With encouragement from many friends and the help of a fellow teacher, Robert Campbell, I made a video displaying my work with Princess, *Princess! The Signing Horse: Whinny*. A photographer for Discovery's Animal Planet came to the ranch and interviewed us for three hours, every minute of which Princess showed off everything asked for (except the lie down). She ended the filming by "eating" the camera. The tape plays on Discovery's Animal Planet's *Amazing Animals*.

Several years earlier, I had contemplated the usefulness of teaching dogs to learn and use their own expanded, gestural language to communicate the details of their perceptions and thoughts. But seeing Princess signing on television sparked me to get started teaching dogs to sign. Dogs already were used for a variety of work, from sniffing drugs, guns, animals, and cancers, as well as sensing, in some mode, seizures and people's thoughts. I immersed myself in dog literature, talked with many canine professionals, observed dog events, various rescue organizations, and researched dog learning and training, breeds and breeders, and visited friends with dogs. I have had, or cared for, dogs at various times in my life, so I knew how well they learned.

I examined and attempted to teach simple gestures to various dogs—some old, some puppies, others deaf—while narrowing down breed options. I considered and visited with poodles, Great Danes, Labradors, Border collies, toy breeds, pugs, Yorkies, and many mixed breeds. I considered rescues and visited local rescues, AFRP and SPCAs. I wanted all the dogs, but had to start somewhere. As a youth, I had cared for a neighbor's shepherd who had left a lasting, respectful, impression on me. It was this memory that led me to choose a German shepherd. I talked with several organizations, settling on one that bred police/working dogs in Santa Cruz, California. Just before Christmas 2003, I brought home Chal, a four-month old friendly and exuberant puppy, the last of the litter. We were perfect for each other, and we both had a lot to learn.

I continued to observe dog behavior and communication at events, in homes, on television. I often left these events aware the dogs were practicing well-known procedural skills, but lacking the cognitive challenges that interested me. The dogs were rewarded for doing what they were told, or for *not* doing something. Some professional dogs are trained to think, to make decisions, including when to disobey (intelligent disobedience) and when to alert their human companions to something in the environment, and we reward them for that. But what were these dogs thinking during the events? Were they bored? What would, or could, these dogs say to us, if we taught them extended language? I was preoccupied with these questions as I taught my high school and college students. I contrasted the human versus canine capability and opportunity to learn and use language. Spending hours teaching humans, many who needed language assistance, I wondered how dogs would fare, if we spent as much time teaching them language, too.

Teachers know that teacher (and parent) expectations affect the outcome of human students' learning. I've seen this firsthand. If this also applies to dog students, it is no wonder they don't "talk" or sign back to us. As a teacher I am particularly sensitive to a look of "desire to communicate but don't know how." My human students who lacked English skills had this look when they wanted to communicate, but didn't know how. I have seen a similar look in many dog's faces. It bothers me. In these humans and dogs, I saw a huge educational gap—illiteracy, but not inability. Dogs can obey, perform wonderful work, problem solve, think on their own, perform intelligent disobedience, and communicate in simple ways. Watch Nature, Discovery, and Animal Planet programs for examples of their intelligence and capabilities. I believe dogs have the potential to learn even more productive language, perhaps even real language. I am determined to try to teach them, and see what they learn and do with this developed skill.

If dogs can sense something (and they can sense a lot), they should be able to express what they sense—in detail. But they don't have the developed skills (that we know about) that work best with their body structure. So, I set forth to create K9Sign for dogs, as I had created EquineSign for horses.

Thus began my adventure creating, researching, and teaching horses and more recently dogs their very own gestural, sign language. I wrote this book to share with you my perspective on animal language acquisition and to introduce you to AnimalSign Language. The step-by-step instructions for introducing K9Sign Language to the dogs in your life include teaching strategies and lessons for the K9Sign Gestuary, milestones and challenges to look out for along the way, tips to help you through them, as well as relevant studies and many of the anecdotal experiences arising from my exploration of helping animals communicate.

The ultimate, academic goal of teaching AnimalSign Language is for the animals to use signs with meaning. The practical aim is to have the animals learn signing as a useful communication tool that has purpose in their lives. As they use, master, and creatively adapt K9Sign for their unique lives, perhaps they will use it as true language. A true language has certainly worked for humans! We should share a true language, fully, with our animal companions. Thus, I offer K9Sign for dogs.

Terminology

To help you understand the terminology and symbols used with Animal-Signing, I've explained their use and definitions in the paragraphs below.

The terms **communication, language,** and **true language** have different meanings in this book. The word **communication** refers to the exchange of information through any method. For animals, this communication might be exchanged vocally, physically, and chemically. For example, a dog wants you to scratch her back, so she leans her back against your hand. The communication is obvious; nothing symbolic here.

The word **language** refers to communicating through learned, arbitrary symbols. For animals this communication would use associatively learned moves as symbols for meanings. For example, if a K9Signing dog wants water, she would place her left paw to her left jaw. The arbitrary moves, gestures, and signs of AnimalSign Language are organized around rules. The term **true language** refers to the rigorous, scientific definition of language. The simple definition for "true language" is that it is an organized, rule-based system of gestures that stand for something (e.g., concepts, objects, actions, feelings, etc.). Gestures have symbolic meaning that can reference, in standard or creative ways, something that is or is not present. With these qualities, the gestures become signs—symbols representing something.

The words **move, gesture,** and **sign** all refer to K9Signs or to natural body language, but each has slightly different meaning. The word **move** indicates a simple body movement. This could be a leg lifted up, or a head tilt. Though **gesture** occasionally refers to any movement that appears to be used for communication, most often it's used to indicate a move that has become associated with a meaning. This might be a leg lift associated with food.

The term **meaving** is a word I developed to refer to the process of graduating a move into a gesture. A gesture purposefully used for communication or language evolves into a **sign.** Gestures may, or not yet, be used symbolically, but signs could be used symbolically, and thus may involve true language.

Instead of using quotation marks to mark the thoughts and communicated words or sentences (on the part of both humans and dogs), I use a first letter capital and all letters in bold italics. This should aid reading the text.

The terms **sign/say** and **objects/events** mean sign and say; objects and/or events respectively. It is shorter and seems simpler to note these with a slash. I explain the exact meaning in the appropriate sections in the book.

Gender does not play a role in the ease of learning K9Sign language. For the sake of simplicity and convenience, and because both my dogs are female, I refer to dogs throughout the text as "she." With respect and care, I refer to all wonderful animals as she, he, they, students, pets, partners, communicators, and companions.

Throughout this book, I share many signing moments I have experienced with Chal, and with my other students at the AnimalSign Center, California State University Monterey Bay (CSUMB), AnimalSign workshops, Signing Socials, as well as some of the signing stories conveyed to me from my clients, friends, and network. Your dog might have the potential of communicating with you through true language, if you would only give her a chance, and teach her. In chapter 10, The Future of Signing Animals, I include imaginary signing events that assume the continued amazing development of canine language potential. Clearly it will take years to study and use signing to see if these can come to fruition. Reread these signing moments often, to remind yourself of what might be possible through K9Sign, and to share the delight of communicating and bonding with animals.

AnimalSigning is happening right now. As the founder of the Animal-Sign Center, I've taught K9Sign Language to numerous dogs and their human companions. With the help of this book, I hope you and your dog will soon be communicating with each other at a level beyond what you thought possible.

CHAPTER 1

AnimalSign Language

K9Sign Language is more than an idea. It is a communication tool that is researched, taught, and practiced at the AnimalSign Center, located in Monterey County, California. Dogs and their people come to the center to learn how to communicate with each other through signs. Learning to sign provides dogs and humans with the opportunity to communicate clearly, for function and fun, at home or at work. Through K9Sign Language, the relationship between dogs and their guardians, caretakers, pet sitters, and trainers is profoundly enhanced. Think about how communication strengthens your human relationships. Why not do the same with your dog? The potential is there, you just have to help your dog communicate better by recognizing her natural signs, and by showing her how to sign to you.

Outside the Center, dogs are already learning how to communicate with us through simple movements such as sitting, barking, nudging, alerting, and looking. Many make requests with simple moves such as door tapping to indicate a desire to go out. Some learning on the part of animals has been taught, while other efforts to communicate seem instinctual. Dogs who are trained to assist hearing-impaired humans often come to recognize and respond to many oral or signed words on their own. Many scientists, trainers, teachers, and enthusiasts have contributed to the education of animals for service, sport, and pleasure. With our help, dogs learn obedience, agility, tracking, search and rescue, assistance, and other remarkable skills. And dogs are not the only animals who learn from humans. Horses learn tricks, dressage, roping, and service skills. Animals learn, learn, learn. We even try to prevent animals from learning certain skills because we don't want them to become bad habits (from our point of view). All these actions are mere fragments of what animals might be capable of doing; we have tapped only the surface of their cognitive abilities and skills. By providing them with a language tool, such as K9Sign Language, we might not only learn about their cognition, but just imagine what they might learn.

Expressing Details

Dogs are aware of many details about the world that humans are not. They smell, see, and hear things we don't. With natural body language, they can grossly express their perceptions. Yet they have no specific way to express their detailed perceptions, thoughts, and desires to us. It is up to us to know dogs well enough to make educated guesses.

Dogs can be trained to identify cancer cell odors for both late and early stage lung and breast cancer, but the dogs communicate only by sitting next to the vial holding the cells they were asked to identify. Imagine if these dogs learned four K9Signs: *Early Lung Cancer, Late Lung Cancer, Early Breast Cancer, Late Breast Cancer.* With this the dogs could identify on a human or animal subject which stage and disease was present on one person, rather than being asked to answer with a sit when they smell any cancer. Dogs could be specific. Without the tools to be *specific and elaborate,* animals can't communicate the details. With the tools, the animals could communicate details we can't perceive ourselves.

Often animals move and vocalize in an effort to communicate something they know. We may understand the general idea, but not the details of what they are saying. Their natural body language only suggests their trains of thought and feelings. How frustrating to have such limited vocabulary (sit, stand, down, bark, growl, paw, dig, look) when they seem to have so much more to say. We can observe and reason, but only guess what dogs are communicating. Some professionals, such as dog language experts Roger Abrantes and Stanley Coren, surely read these animals better than others.

But even their translations may be indirect or inaccurate. Animals might be capable of much more elaborate communication. With additional language skills, dogs could directly tell us what they are "saying," and we could understand and respond.

Some people state they can sense, using some invisible, unmeasurable stimuli, then intuit, translate, and understand what animals are thinking. Some people, with their perceptions and interpretations of animal behavior, using a variety of techniques, have much to contribute to our understanding animal cognition. This book does not delve into those other techniques, but I do value sharing and pooling our diverse methods, resources, and knowledge to better understand and communicate with our animals.

If animals have the cognitive ability to know what they are trying to say, why can't they directly, visibly tell us in detail? Because they have no organized, agreed-upon language other than a few natural body gestures learned during socialization. They lack a tool, a code, to *precisely* map their thoughts into visible signs. We haven't taught them a method of communicating *details* in a visible or oral form that we can interpret. As much as we observe and spend time with them, as many treats we offer and tricks we engage them in, we have not yet taught dogs an expanded *productive* language (language that is produced). We leave their communication skills natural, but undeveloped; we leave them illiterate. Would we leave our human children in such a limited state?

What kind of productive language might be useful teach animals? One that is made for and customized for animal bodies and minds; one that includes signs for humans to communicate to animals, but specifically focuses on signs for the animals to communicate to humans. Animals, such as dogs and horses can't vocalize as extensively as we do and they can't fingerspell (not yet, anyway). Ah! But they can move their many body parts in various combinations and patterns, in space and in time! They have a natural body language to seed this learning. This mobility and the ability to learn are the foundations of AnimalSign Language—and specifically K9Sign Language for dogs.

Having a language ready to teach is one thing; learning it is another. Dogs have inborn mechanisms that enable them to learn, problem solve, and perform simple communications. Can dogs learn a simple language, or our type of true language? Can they learn a language that can be divided into receptive and productive components? Receptive language focuses on the understanding of the meaning of signed, written, or spoken words. Productive refers to producing words, for example by gesturing or vocalizing. There is documented and anecdotal evidence for dogs receptively learning language. Animals seem to understand what we say, sign, and possibly write. They run to the door when they hear the word "walk," and grab their favorite ball when they see people gesture *Play,* and on seeing a street sign with the written word STOP, a dog for the blind will stop.

Researched evidence in this area is growing. Dogs have learned some receptive oral, signed, and written language. They understand our many languages, our spoken words, visible signs, and a few of our written words. Recently a particularly talented dog named Rico who understands two hundred spoken words was tested by animal psychologist Juliane Kaminski and others, and commented on by Paul Bloom in *Science* (June 2004). Dr. Bonita Bergin, founder of Canine Companions for Independence, has attempted to teach dogs to read (and posted YouTube videos) at the Assistance Dog Institute in California.

Capacity for Language?

Do dogs have the capacity to learn a productive language or true language? A few dog experts acknowledge we just don't know; we haven't tried or tested this ability scientifically. Virtually all others say or assume the answer is no. They don't consider the possibility. Why? I suggest this attitude is prevalent because dogs aren't already talking, writing, and producing language (other than natural body language). The assumed inability to learn a nonnatural language comes also from the idea that these animals don't have the appropriate body type for expressing this type of language. When considering productive language, the focus is usually on the voice, though the whole body is available. Some scientists might claim dogs don't have the cognition, the innate skills, or the instinct to produce language. Otherwise, they'd already be creating and learning a language on their own. But don't animals living together in stable groups for long periods of time build common vocabulary onto their existing body language? For animals such as chimpanzees, this type of expanded communication has been clearly documented by Dr. Jane

Goodall and others. Perhaps other animals are able to do the same thing. We should continue to watch the animals in our lives, carefully, for added vocabulary.

Along with possible cognition issues, dogs have a huge physical challenge (from a human perspective). They are, necessarily, on their movable limbs all day, and their voices appear to have limited use for expanded language (in the range we can hear). (Perhaps, with a human professional voice trainer, they could learn to produce many more specific sounds.) In contrast, we humans are only on two of our limbs and use the other two for manipulations and language. We have our hands and voice available for communication anytime.

A glaring omission in animal literature is the perception of dogs as potential productive language learners. The idea that we can teach them productive language is absent. Experts are busy productively focusing on developing a dog's known talents and skills. Many see what dogs have done and can now do, rather than what they could do. In much of this literature, I can't help but read these phrases between the lines: "Dogs can't learn language because their brains are too small." "Wrong body type." "They can't produce language because they don't have a vocal apparatus, or hands, like ours." "They can't because they haven't." "They can't because they don't."

While it is true that dogs have different brains than humans, animals and humans also have many similar, core anatomical structures (hypothalamus, temporal and frontal lobes, limbic and sensory systems) involved in learning, anticipation, emotions, and feelings. We haven't yet sufficiently explored the cognitive function of animal language neuroanatomy. (It would be fascinating to compare the neuroanatomy of canine identical siblings as one is taught language and the other is not.) Canine brains aren't as convoluted, nor is their cortex as large as ours. But those are not the only determinant wirings of language capability. Dogs are very skilled at anticipation and detection of subtle cues. These animals also have more sensitive, neuroanatomical structures, when it comes to smell, movement detection, and some aspects of hearing and vision. (How, I wonder, do their brains cognitively network a map of their expansive sense of smell?)

With these and other similarities, some level of anthropomorphism (in reference to learning and feeling systems) is appropriate. While the sophistication and networking capabilities of these systems do differ from ours, and thus, we might expect some differences in extent of ability. It would be fascinating to uncover the extent of similarities and differences while attempting to teach language. In the end—and most importantly—although many animals have picked up receptive language on their own, we have not taught them productive language. So, whatever we think of their anatomical differences, we really don't know what they could do—if taught. That potential for language learning is what we are exploring at the AnimalSign Center.

The expectation that dogs can learn productive language isn't there for most people. Many have just accepted and become used to perceiving dogs as nonlanguage learners. Or perhaps some see dogs only as receptive learners, but not as articulate, language producers. As a teacher, I take a different approach. I will presume dogs can learn language, until they provide evidence they can't. If a human child isn't learning at school, we should not immediately come to the conclusion that the student can't learn. The student could be in the wrong class, with the wrong teacher, using the wrong book, being taught with the wrong method. My hypothesis with animals is that they aren't learning productive language, or true language, because we haven't taught them. If we try to teach language to animals and they don't learn, we would still need to consider that this failing could be ours. We may not be teaching with the appropriate methods or under the right conditions. Perhaps they may not be learning because we are using the wrong language structure for them. Many other reasons could exist. Only as a last answer should we consider that animals simply can't learn true language, as we define and teach it. I presume that students (regardless of the body, the [dis]abilities, and the conditions) can learn. I take it upon myself to find ways to make learning happen. I take this same approach to animals—dogs in particular.

Let's give our canine companions the opportunity to try to learn, and see what they do with true language education. There is everything to gain and nothing to lose (except the belief that true language is the private domain of primates and birds). If dogs learn language, it may not be as sophisticated as ours, but it might be sufficiently different to warrant a new line of questioning, investigating, and thinking when it comes to language and animals. We just don't know, yet.

While attempting to teach signing to animals, I have seen horses and dogs learn new gestures linked and associated in some way to a specific object, such as a ball or brush. A dog might spontaneously sign **Ball,** meaning she wants to play with it, a horse might sign **Brush,** meaning she wants to be brushed. (Later in this book you will learn how to test that your animal understands meaning.) These behaviors need not be commanded, nor cued. These gestures appear to represent something meaningful to them (food, toy, play, water, open door). I have seen animals communicate with these newly learned gestures. Chal, my German shepherd, has gestured with her food paw (not her toy paw) when I showed her new foods that she had never seen. She has also used the sign *Toy* for my cat before she learned to sign *Cat.* Chal has spontaneously made up her own sign and her own move to convey a message to me. She lifted her right paw and bent it toward me to convey (what I interpreted) as *Teach Me the Sign.* These gestures are a step, but they do not mean that Chal or other animals that use gestures have learned a structured language. But this step is encouraging enough for me to continue teaching and testing human and animal—human-animal—teams. With many teams working, we can accumulate and share more data to get an indication of whether animals can learn or are learning signs, a language, or a formal language. If dogs are not using gestures as signs, for true language, then what *are* they doing? I aim to understand their use of K9Sign wherever it takes me, physically and intellectually.

Clever Hans

Canine and equine cognition research reveals that animals can do much more than we previously imagined. Some experts are actively researching and discussing how dogs might be outpacing nonhuman primates in certain cognitive skills. Some research suggests that dogs are better than wolves and chimpanzees at tracking our glances. Many people have wondered and (some inappropriately) tested whether horses, dogs, and birds can count with numbers and can creatively problem solve. Though many dog and horse owners think their animals can count, this claim remains to be critically tested. Doubt stems from the Clever Hans Phenomenon (CHP), which any claim of capability in animals needs to address.

Clever Hans was a horse trained by a school teacher to perform a variety of feats, including counting. When tested by others, however, Hans was found to be responding to cues from the knowing audience rather than coming up with the answers himself. CHP refers to the handler's, teacher's, or audience's inadvertent influence on the tested behavior of an animal. In other words, the animal may not have learned what the teacher thought he was teaching. But instead the animal may have accidentally (or purposefully!) been taught to respond to a cue from the audience. For example, if a handler "taught" then asked a dog to count to five, the dog might bark to five, and then stop for many reasons that have nothing to do with counting. The dog may stop barking when it hears the audience hold its breath in anticipation, or when the handler (knowingly or not) does something with his body, or says "Good Boy" right at five barks. The animal may sense the handler is nervous and emitting a particular odor at the fifth bark. Anything a dog can sense can be an inadvertent cue. The dog may have learned to stop barking when sensing any of these cues. Of course, chance (guessing) can factor into all this as well. The dog may have been trained (or trained himself) to observe a particular nonnumeric cue and found it rewarding. Was the dog trained to see the number 5 and count, or to cue off something else that happened to appear regularly when the correct number was present? It is all in the training.

Double-blind studies would need to be performed to tell us what is really happening here. This is where no one present knows (even unconsciously) the correct answer, except—one hopes—the dog. Computers with randomizing number display programs that make identical sounds and identical screen displays except for the number are very useful for this type of test. The problem with CHP lies in the teaching, not the student. Hans was surely clever, but his teacher was not!

Natural Language

Have animals already come up with their own extended languages, ones we don't notice? Dogs do have a basic natural language that we humans have recognized and documented (for more on this subject read Roger Abrantes' and Stanley Coren's books on animal behavior and intelligence). But beyond this natural language, dogs haven't appeared to have created an extended language. If animals are making up detailed gestures or signs for us that we don't recognize and respond to accordingly, they'll stop using the gestures. Even if they have created signs, how would they pass them on to others in an effective way? By bark-of-mouth?

Those observing dogs and horses in stable groups for years at a time might be able to record new moves and vocalizations from these animals. The potential for an elephant language is particularly interesting to consider because of the elephant's long lifespan and the relationships these animals build within the herd. But most animals we encounter don't live together long enough to build a solid, extensive, structured language that they can pass on to their pack or herd. They change households, ranches, stalls, and shelters so often that communicating standard meanings and building an extensive language would be difficult. Animals that do live in groups for long periods of time undoubtedly build up a repertoire of communication gestures. Scientists are studying this phenomenon in various species. But our findings are limited by our inability to observe, to sense, and perceive the details of animal interactions over long periods of time We surely miss much. Animals naturally learn some of our many human languages on a receptive level; they understand much of what we say and sign. In fact, they are somewhat literate in receptive language—and perhaps more literate in understanding our body language than we are. There is growing interest in testing and documenting these anecdotal observations.

The natural body gestures dogs offer, and the signs they have learned to recognize from us and each other, appear to be instinctual—it happens naturally. But they don't appear to be creating and using a more humanlike elaborate language—considered to be an instinctual process for us. Why? We don't know. I propose a few possibilities. Dogs may not have the developed brain circuitry in the relevant cognitive areas that are designed for elaborate language. They may not have the *idea* of building a language system. They are also certainly hindered by the lack of flexible voice mechanisms to create various sounds, a lack of free limbs to move around for signing, and for many, a lack social circles and civilization resources that facilitate language expansion. We certainly don't help the situation. We control their world and tell them what to do; if they try to tell us what they'd like to do, often we are taught to *not* respond. For example, a trainer might reinforce a human's leadership role over her dogs by not allowing the dogs to initiate certain behaviors. On a walk the human directs the path and speed, the dog should follow. The dog should sit, until the human releases the dog. Some trainers recommend that people feed or play with dogs only when the human decides to feed or play. In some cases, this is for good manners, guidance, safety, convenience, but even for simple control. We, not they, must initiate the desired behavior or interaction. By restricting an animal's ability to initiate, we reduce their motivation to pursue language creation. They likely have tried to teach us more of their natural language, but as we don't get it, and focus instead on teaching them obedience, animals quit trying. Especially for behaviors we want to limit, we encourage them *not* to communicate what they'd like to do, but to do as we ask. Even if we teach our dogs K9Sign, when they give us the natural play gesture (a pounce of the upper body to the ground, with hind up) to play, we may believe it is up to us to decide when it's time to play. So, we don't play. The ***Play*** gesture then comes to mean ***Don't Play.*** We inadvertently de-motivate, and promote their *not* communicating with us.

Exceptions to this rule are the alerting and rescue dogs who are taught to communicate with us under certain situations. That type of communication is useful, but broad and limited. A dog may learn to alert the handler to an alarm clock, rather than sign details such as ***Alarm, 4 o'clock.*** A dog may alert to the phone ringing rather than express details ***Phone, Mary*** (meaning the phone rang, the answering machine is on, and that it recognizes Mary's voice talking).

Currently these dogs learn to alert the handler to an alarm clock or to the phone ringing, by running back and forth from the object to the person, or in some cases to bring the movable object to the person. But if they could also be taught to sign, they could give their handlers details such as ***Alarm, 4 o'clock,*** and ***Phone, Mary*** (meaning the phone rang, the answering machine is on, and the dog recognizes Mary's voice is talking).

Dogs can communicate naturally by pointing to or touching objects to indicate preferences. Penny Patterson and I exchange gesturing or signing experiences with our dogs (and Penny with Koko the gorilla). Penny's dog Rikki Power naturally gestures in a variety of situations, and Penny keenly observes and readily responds to her. For example, Rikki will indicate a cupboard that contains a variety of dog foods and biscuits. When Penny asks her what she wants, Rikki often will select up to three different choices. This way

Rikki no longer needs to select foods individually and return to the cupboard three times, she selects once and gets all three choices.

This type of natural gesturing provides a great opportunity to introduce signing to your pet. After reinforcing the choice(s) your dog communicates (chicken-flavored biscuit), make use of that selected interest immediately by teaching her to sign *Chicken.* Doing this will empower her (at your expense) to tell you, from anywhere in the house, that she wants chicken. In other words, you can inspire interest in signing by letting your dog point to what she wants, then teach her the sign for it.

No Communication

Negation of communication is extensively used when training horses. We are often trained to *not* respond if the horse communicates something it wants or needs. We are taught to ignore its communicative behavior. A horse on a trail ride who indicates *I Want to Go to My Paddock* by heading toward the barn is turned around and *not* allowed to go to the barn. This is done so that the horse understands she doesn't make the decisions, the rider does. But also, so that the horse doesn't learn that by heading back to barn means she gets to go back—we don't want to reinforce this particular form of communication. We do the opposite. If we didn't, we'd be stuck riding in the barn (where the horse wants to be) or from the ground (after being bucked off). There are safety reasons for doing this. A horse that doesn't want to leave the barn may communicate that by bucking the rider off, or not leaving the barn. (I recommend communicating to the horse that she can do what she wants later, but for now, you ask that she cooperate, and she will be rewarded. Regularly reward the horse after each ride with carrots and some time in a favorite pasture. If the horse really is adverse to what you are asking, and won't change, consider other options for her.)

When the horse learns that her expressed desire to go back to the barn results in the outcome of *not* going back to the barn, communication is stalled, and becomes a maze to unravel. (Imagine how you would react, if when you told a friend you wanted something, your friend would be sure you didn't get it. You'd probably create a contorted way to maneuver getting what you wanted. In some cases, this is the state of animal-human communication.

For safety, of course, cutting off or ignoring some communication is reasonable and understandable. But from a language-learning perspective, it really twists up gestures and meanings or outcomes, and truly dislocates the purpose of communication. An empathetic and sophisticated handler will know when to listen, encourage, and respond to communications and when to discourage and ignore them. The overall message from us is clear: "do not communicate." I call this discouraging training NOCom.

One exception to this type of training is used with animals who are taught to alert—to bark or nudge you when something needs your attention. This is part of the assistance, search and rescue (SAR), and other training programs. Alerting is a great place to start language training. The animal finds it worthwhile to communicate via alerting. For practical communication purposes, whether an animal learns language on its own or is taught is irrelevant. We humans wouldn't be as far along with language if we had been left to learn it without help from each other. I believe we need to research and teach select animals a detailed gestural language. We need to teach them in a form they can cognitively understand and physically perform, with the anticipated outcome of expanded communication—animal literacy—as the focus.

No Expectations

Why, when dogs have lived with us for so long have we not taught them productive language before? For many reasons. We have not had the *expectation* that dogs might learn and use a new, extensive, gestural language. We have not had an available structured language system useful to both people and dogs. We have taught them to recognize many human gestures (commands to them) and a few gestures to make to alert us. Alerting is communication, but not language, and certainly not a language dogs can use to extensively sign to us. Our reluctance to develop a dog's ability to communicate to us through language might also be due to our respect for their natural body language (observe and understand it, but don't change it). We are also preoccupied with our own goals for dogs, training them in obedience, agility, sport, farming, and other skills. These are very time consuming.

When I met my horse Princess in 1994, I was preoccupied and obsessed with communicating with her. This took all my spare time from work and school. Only after a few years with Princess, did I consider teaching dogs. It took a few years more years after that to find the right dog and explore methods of teaching her language. Teaching language takes time. Many parents and guardians have difficulty trying to schedule enough time for their human children.

We humans are provided much support while teaching language to the others of our species. We have expectations that humans will learn and use language. We have many languages premade for our various abilities (vocal, auditory, visual, written, sign, etc.). We have regular and special schools (with specially trained teachers) for teaching true language. We expect to dedicate *years* to the development of language. Imagine where we would be without that training investment and that support! Dogs are without just that.

Inherent in K9Sign Language is the open expectation that, with the right teaching strategies, dogs will learn the gestures, the signs, communications, and perhaps, real language. To facilitate these right conditions, human teachers need to prioritize and plan lessons and practice sessions on a regular basis. It takes time and patience. Before teaching language, understand how to teach, and then you and your dog need to understand basic obedience tasks. The K9Sign Language is divided into the Human K9Signs and the Canine K9Signs. The Canine signs are divided into Basic/Foundation, Intermediate, and Advanced signs. Just as with baby signing, seeing signing happen can takes weeks to months depending on the age, animal, and teacher. After studying this book, I expect you will have the conceptual and practical knowledge, as well as beginning tools, to start teaching your dogs to "communicate" to you in K9Sign Language. Try to keep up with them!

Language Support

AnimalSign Center offers various support resources for teaching and learning to communicate with animals, including private tutoring, education, training, live and tele-seminars, human and animal workshops (crash or series), books, upcoming videos and DVDs. I provide AnimalSign classes, K9Sign certification, and canine biology and behavior courses at the Center and at CSUMB. At graduation, the animals receive certificates acknowledging the signs learned. People (trainers, educators, enthusiasts) who are interested in seriously pursuing AnimalSign (K9Sign or EquineSign) can obtain the AnimalSign Language Education Certificate. These participants would take select Animal Biology, Behavior, and Cognition (Intelligence and Language) courses (through CSUMB and E-Trainingfordogs.com) along with the AnimalSign course series.

Educator certification is important to maintain the language standards so that people and animals everywhere can communicate using the same signs. This consistency also opens the possibility of canine-to-canine K9Signing. As I teach clients, their animals, and my own animals, it has been useful to receive feedback from human and animal students. I encourage human clients and students to stay in contact by phone, by email, blog response, tele-seminars, online groups, and upcoming conferences. In the Carmel and Monterey area Signing Socials (parties for people and animals), occur several times a year to allow signers to get together and exchange animal stories, communications, challenges, and milestones. I attend these and give suggestions to promote communication. In addition to networking with signers, the Center recruits or exchanges with educators, scientists, biology and Vet Tech students for various signing research and activities.

By explaining to you how to teach a gestural language to dogs, I seek to empower them to communicate in details. Using gestures or signs, anytime, anywhere, they may take their language with them—on a search and rescue, or a friendly visit. With this language, dogs have the opportunity to create new terms on the go. Though other methods (pointing boards and lexigrams) may be useful, they limit the location where signing can happen, as well as limit the creative opportunities for dogs to make their own signs. With a structured, rule-based gestural language, dogs have an enhanced opportunity to grow and share their knowledge and world with us. I wonder what each signing dog will describe.

Now I encourage you to expect more language from your dogs; view them as untrained, not unable; illiterate, not incapable. K9Sign Language, a made-for-animal, friendly, gestural language awaits you and your animal's use. The power of this new perspective and tool is in the bodies and minds of skilled enthusiasts, scientists, trainers, teachers, and animal students. Join us on this journey!

CHAPTER 2

K9Sign Language

AnimalSign Language has two main forms (at this time), one for dogs and one for horses. In this book, I focus on the CanineSign Language, also known as K9Sign Language, but the languages operate on the same principle—as a learned communication tool for animals to visibly communicate, extending their natural body language. Animals learn to move their bodies in certain ways to communicate certain things. The language consists of an organized system of body gestures, using rules for moves and meanings. The rules are easily learned by humans and animals. Animals may use the rules to make up new gestures that humans or animals might guess the meaning of. Is AnimalSign language a true language (an organized, rule-based system of gestures that stand for something), or is it a simple communication tool? Each of the AnimalSign Languages are designed to be able to be used a true language, but whether animals will do so needs to be determined. In this chapter, I discuss both the difference between communication and language and also our basic understanding of animal gestures. I discuss the cautious usefulness of anthropomorphism (attributing human characteristics to animal behavior) in studying animal behavior and language.

AnimalSign is a *learned* language used by animals and humans to communicate. It is more than just the animal's natural body language, which are the natural gestures animals make, sometimes to communicate. At this point, let me remind you of the distinction between the meanings of the three words: **move, gesture,** and **sign.** A **move** refers to a particular observable (change in) position of a body part, such as a paw move up. A **gesture** refers to a move that is associated with a meaning, though it may, or may not, be an attempt to communicate, such as a dog raising its paw when you put your hand out. The move is the paw moving up (alone), but this becomes a gesture since it is associated with, or has some meaning related to, your hand being out. The dog could simply be responding (to the cue of your hand) or communicating (hold my paw). Some meaning is associated with this gesture. A **sign** (as in K9Sign) is a gesture that communicates, potentially as a language symbol, A symbol is something (such as a word or object) that represents something else, such as the word "food" symbolizing actual food. Notice that the word gesture emphasizes the move associated with a meaning, and the word "sign" emphasizes the meaning associated with a gesture. With AnimalSign Language, animals must learn to make certain moves, which then become gestures when the animals learn the meanings associated with the moves. The gestures may be used as a simple form of communication, but they are designed to be used as signs—symbols that refer to various concepts—which is the basis of true language with all its complexities. The gestures are taught in a specific way to promote the use of gestures as signs, as language. Whether animals will do this to the extent required of true language is not yet known, but AnimalSign language makes it possible to examine this.

AnimalSign language has rules for the body gestures used as signs and their meanings. The meanings of the gestures, the signs, are mapped to the animal's body part and sides, as well as to position, placement, movement, pattern, repetition, timing, in context. The language is rule-based and logical, with standardized moves. This makes it easier for an animal to learn, use creatively, and elaborate, and for us to study. For example, of the three possible signs for *Potty* (back legs form a wide stance, spinning in circles, ring a special bell), your dog may find it easiest to move a hind leg out to a wide stance. For creative use, an animal shown a new food will likely move its *left* paw (food sign leg), and might move that paw in a new creative manner, thus making up a new sign herself, following the learned rules. Communication and language are possible when agreed-upon rules and symbols are used. The animal gestures in specific ways to refer to specific concepts or objects that may not even be present. An animal lifting its left paw up high and then down refers to ***Chicken.*** This chicken may be hidden in a cabinet.

Though AnimalSign Language currently has two main sublanguages, K9Sign for dogs and EquineSign for horses, other animals may also use a sublanguage modified for their body and skill. The language gestures can accommodate customized signs for each animal group, allowing some language-rule exceptions. English is filled with exceptions, but this also makes it difficult to learn as a second language. To avoid this difficulty, AnimalSign minimizes exceptions. To maintain the AnimalSign Language standard and to maximize animal-to-people, animal-to-animal communication, I created Gestuaries, dictionaries of gestures. These Gestuaries are constantly growing. In this dog book, I provide the K9Sign Gestuary. In my next book, the Equine Gestuary will be included.

As people and animals learn the language, they will more easily be understood by other signers, anytime, anywhere. Imagine a dog from California using natural body language and K9Signs to communicate with a dog from New York, England, France, or Asia!

The general public refers to communication as language, with animal communication generally interpreted as language. This means that a dog pushing a toy into a person's leg is considered communicating, or using language, to say she wants to play. But to some experts this act is only communication, maybe a use of language, but not a true language. In this book, I use communication to mean expressing something naturally obvious (to at least one of the participants), as the dog pushing the toy did. I use the term "language" in two ways. "Language" (without "true") is a simple communication form that uses gestures apparently as signs to express thoughts. This type of communication is responsive but generally not spontaneous. For example, a dog might respond to your request to identify something like a toy or person. Or a dog might bring a person her water dish when she wants water. She communicates in an obvious way, but this is not using language. I use the words "true language" to refer to communications that use gestures as signs—symbols. These symbols refer in a nonobvious way to something that may be present or out of sight. Many other requirements for true language exist. The scientific, rigorous definition of true language requires more than animals using gestures as symbolic communication; it requires the use of gestures as symbols (signs), with meanings that refer to concepts not present. In addition to numerous other requirements, these signs must be used in ways not specifically taught. People who don't learn a formal language can still use natural gestures (pointing or pushing), but linguists do not consider those gestures as formal language.

The following example might be a candidate for true language. A dog comes upstairs and uses the K9Sign for **Water** (lifts her left front leg up to touch her paw to her mouth) to her person. The person only says **Show Me,** and the dog walks downstairs to the water dish and gestures **Water** again. The person only says **Where IS It?** and the dog walks over to the sink putting her paws on the knob. Did the dog conceptualize that the sign for **Water** meant water? Could the dog just have known that gesturing **Water** would result in her person getting water? Certainly further imaginative and critical exploration is needed to interpret what dogs are thinking as they gesture or sign. The fun of it all.

Since we have not (on a grand scale) taught a formal, gestural language to dogs, we don't know whether they can learn a true language. I see dogs learning and spontaneously using the gestures and signs in intelligent ways. We have not ruled out the possibility that they might indeed learn true language. Let's not flunk them before we teach them in home school, at work, or in language school!

Whether AnimalSign Language meets the criteria for a possible true language is not the focus of this introductory book. Teaching, gathering, and interpreting data to support or refute the idea that these animals can use formal language surely is a lifelong process. It involves many students (human and animal), guardians, and scientists and many pilots, trials, tests, and reflections. This adventure stirs up many questions: Will these gestures transform into signs, symbols, and tools for communicating in a true sign language? If so, how is the language, the use of signs, similar to or different from ours? Can the signs be used for anything besides true language, and if so, what? How do the teaching methods influence (and limit) the sign development and use? Will teaching K9Sign change and develop a dog's brain, or initiate the development of a more sophisticated language center? Will teaching K9Sign early in a puppy's life promote more profound development and use of K9Sign or other language? What can we unveil about animal cognition with this tool? And what other questions regarding these animals does this perspective unleash?

It has been well documented that animals have some form of communication or language using their own body gestures. (To read more about canine communication, read Roger Abrantes' book *Dog Language*, published in various human languages itself.) Even so, some people believe that nonprimate animals do not have, and cannot learn, a new formal humanlike language. Perhaps brain anatomy can tentatively guide our expectations. In the past, we have not seriously tried to teach productive language to nonprimates (with the exception of some birds). Can we expect animals to develop an expansive productive language such as our children have without some education? Until now, animals have had no formal productive language training to help them elaborate and organize gestural communication, nor have they had access to gestural language schools. Some people have taught a few gestures through home schooling. We might expect that dogs living with signing people might have some similar signs themselves. Hearing dogs are taught to be alert to important sounds. At the Bergin University of Canine Studies (formerly called the Assistance Dog Institute) in Santa Rosa, California, dogs are taught to read letter signs. Recently, as a guest lecturer, I introduced K9Sign Language to their staff. When I demonstrated how to teach signs to their dogs, I found the dogs eager and quick to learn. As this signing journey continues, animals are learning gestures and signs, definitely as tricks and manipulations, surely as communications and language, and just maybe, as true language. Whether gestures are true signs or language, K9Sign use is fun, fulfilling, and useful for animals and humans.

AnimalSign Language includes gestures and their meanings taught in a structured way, with tools and methods, and with associated rules for teaching the language. Teaching the language should be performed in the order explained, with the associated lesson suggestions, to maximize the possibility that the animal will be able to use the signs as a language. It is designed for, and expected to be expanded by, the animals themselves. Animals with specialized professions (that need only a few specific signs) may pick and choose which ones to use, but this selection (from the Intermediate, and Advanced level signs) should occur *after* completing the Basic level signs. This way the students will have the foundation skills to learn any gesture.

The teaching methods used in this book are based on our knowledge of animal and human learning, respectively, for moves and language. The methods focus on positive reinforcement with guided feedback. As humans require different learning strategies, animals will as well. If you already use a preferred method, I hope the information here will enhance or complement your skills. Use what works. For new or difficult gestures, the clicker method is very useful. Using the clicker in conjunction with an exhuberant *Yes!* is a powerful reinforcement of behavior, as it amplifies the effect of *Yes!* even later when used alone.

Comparing how my horse, Princess, and dog, Chal, learn and use gestures is fascinating. Princess is great at imitation, but Chal is sluggish with it. Princess learns on the spot and doesn't forget; Chal takes time to absorb a new lesson. Princess tries creative variations of the moves I model; Chal finds her own unique moves to carry out a communicated goal. Princess and I have worked together for many years; Chal and I only for a few. They are both good at creating new moves, but do so differently. Princess is a ham; Chal appears more thoughtful and careful while problem solving. Princess excels at prompting me to feed and scratch her; Chal succeeds at provoking me to play! It is no wonder that we three mammals, each a different species, have different inclinations, talents, strategies, and needs.

Attempting to teach AnimalSign implies some use of anthropomorphism—more critical than classical. Anthropomorphism is the assignment of humanlike feelings and motivations to nonhuman creatures. Given that many similarities exist in the human, horse, and dog brain and physiology, it is reasonable to hypothesize or assume some low-level anthropomorphic interpretations of behavior and feelings. Feelings are functionally attributed to the limbic system, which all three animals have. This indicates our basic emotions might be similar. However, variations in the brain cortex, where control and integration of higher-level functions are managed, might lead us to expect that emotional development and complexity differ. For example, joy is an emotion or state visible in both the expressions and behavior of the dog and human. In *Dog Language*, joy is listed as a natural dog language expression. We attribute a certain feeling to the joy behaviors we observe, though we have no clear or direct knowledge of the dog's, nor another human's, experience.

To attribute humanlike feelings and perceptions to animals, with respect to similar anatomy and physiology, is an acceptable level of anthropomorphism. (An interesting article by Wendy Van Kerkhove discussing anthropomorphism can be found in Association of Pet Dog Trainers [APDT].) Yet anthropomorphism is a skill that should be used critically while trying to interpret and assess a nonhuman behavior. Used appropriately, the skill can be useful. Consider these two levels of assessing:

Example 1: Say I'm sitting on a couch and see Chal move her left paw up and then down (the sign for *Biscuit*), I say "Show Me." Chal walks, looks back, then waits; she stops and paws the biscuit bin (not the cat food or the lamb bin). I could interpret her behavior by assigning my feelings to her and presume she *wants* a biscuit and was asking me to get it for her. In this assessment I use an anthropomorphic interpretation—suggesting she is doing things as I might, if I were a dog or she a human. But I would be "jumping the bin" by taking an anthropomorphic interpretation and could come to a wrong conclusion. When I saw her move her paw performing *Biscuit,* I might have unconsciously cued her to go to the biscuit bin. I saw her move in what I knew was the *Biscuit* gesture, but she may not have taken me to the biscuit bin had I not cued her to do what I thought she wanted—to go to the biscuit bin.

Example 2: Say I'm slouched on a couch, with my arms blocking any view. Chal comes over and signs *Biscuit* (moves her left paw up and down). This time I don't see her sign but see her eyes looking at me, not knowing to what they refer. She proceeds (looking at and waiting for me) to walk to, then paw, the same biscuit bin. In this case, because I didn't see her paw move I couldn't cue her to the biscuit bin. However, if the scene had been videotaped, I could later watch her sign *Biscuit,* then go to the bin and paw it. In this case, I might be more confident that she signed *Biscuit* and wanted me to get her a biscuit. This would be a relatively safe hypothesis. Other double-blind control tests would need to be done to more surely validate the conclusion. Having an anthropomorphic hypothesis (that animals can learn "our" type of language) is not necessarily erroneous and might be supported by future evidence.

While anthropomorphism has its limitations, its use in AnimalSign Language opens opportunities to share something special—language—with animals. It allows us to examine how similar to, or different from, us animals are in this cognitive process. If animals can use this educational gift as a language, or as even a useful trick, it would be wasteful to deny it to them. If they display specific inabilities or blocks, even to the point of not learning language, these findings will expose their hidden cognitive processes. In addition to my work at the AnimalSign Center, I am a college instructor. While teaching math, life science, and physiology, I learn much about how my human students think when they learn, or don't learn, something. The goal is to understand our animals, whatever their abilities.

AnimalSign Language, in particular K9Sign Language, I structured with a specific design that dogs can understand and elaborate on themselves. Object categories are represented by a body part that is moved in a certain way, within a given context. A gesture or sign is a specific move performed by a specific body part, with the remaining body in a specific configuration, within a given context. One gesture performed in various contexts might represent different meanings.

Most word categories follow anatomical lines:

- Living things are represented by left body-side gestures.

    Foods (once living, now nonliving) by the front left leg.

    Living animals by the hind left leg.

- Inanimate (nonliving) objects are represented by right body-side gestures

    Toys and other smaller movable objects by the right front leg.

    Larger inanimate, immovable objects by the hind right leg.

- Proper names (Mary, Sean, etc.) are represented by moves of the head and neck.

- Adjectives (small, large, colors, etc.) are represented by moves of, and around, head regions.

- Verbs are represented by moves of the trunk and body (moving around, etc.).

- Adverbs and emotional states are represented by tail moves and head gestures. (Tail moves are also reserved for new meanings, not yet assigned.)

The context, environmental variations, locations, movement, and repetition of gestures can also distinguish different meanings. Because different animal groups have different movable body parts, are capable of different movement patterns and locations, and will operate in varying contexts, a separate sign Gestuary exists for horses, dogs, and other animals. Customized gestures are created to accommodate particular animals and their needs.

In *Dog Language*, Abrantes has clearly sketched and described various natural body part (mouth, lips, eyes, ears, head, forehead, paws, etc.) moves (curled, drawn back, slanted, etc.) that we associate with specific meanings (aggression, dominance, submission, invitation to play, etc.). Stanley Coren, author of *The Intelligence of Dogs*, discusses linguistics—natural body language and its possible meanings. Initially a dog would probably use natural body language moves as described in these books to communicate generally, but after learning K9Sign, the dog would have tools to communicate more specifically.

Play is an interesting natural gesture I use in K9Sign to kick-off signing lessons. A dog's natural tendency to extend its forelegs while raising its rear in a play-bow is the basis for the sign *Play*. Its power is that exchanging play-bows engages you and the dog in clear communication. A great place to start signing.

Dogs can also learn to sign another simple play move, in addition to the play-bow. Chal has learned that slapping only her right paw down while slightly dipping her head and back results in me playing with her. She imitated my movement of slapping the floor with my hand. We have now incorporated both the *Play* sign (using right paw down) with the natural play-bow as K9Signs for *Play*.

Sublanguages

AnimalSign Language offers a language for nonprimate animals to use and develop in their lives. Variations of the K9Sign for dogs and EquineSign for horses can be adapted for other animals, including wolves, mules, donkeys, cows, goats, and other similarly structured animals. The languages are most often referred to as AnimalSign, K9Sign (CanineSign), and Equine-Sign (HorseSign). A bird trainer approached me about creating a sublanguage for birds, AvianSign. Of course parrots can vocalize, but for parrots that don't talk, signing could add to their remarkable communications. Any animal capable of learning and moving should be able to use signing to communicate.

The sublanguage forms that I created are affixed with an ASL (Animal-Sign Langauge) title (K9*ASL* and Equine*ASL*) to emphasize their connection with American Sign Language for humans (ASL). K9*ASL* Gestuary is not covered specifically in this book, though a few signs overlap to accommodate dogs, such as the sign **Water.** Some K9Signs might match (for the dog) the signs in K9*ASL* and match to some extent the human American Sign Language signs. American Sign Language is in part a basis for K9Sign, and more so for K9*ASL*. Some people using American Sign Language have devised special signs to communicate with their dogs, and are often keenly observant of their dog's body language. By request, I do create customized signs for the sublanguage versions for dogs with special needs to accommodate their relationship and situation. For example, one person with a service dog had proposed creating a sign so her dog could tell her *why* he wanted to leave a building quickly. Was it the noise, the lights, the air, or that the dog needed to urinate? I hope these additional language resources will expand existing communication and improve relationships and mutual caretaking.

Using K9*ASL,* conceivably a dog could sign to an ASL-savvy person who would have the language background to guess what the dog is communicating. This could be useful for assistance dogs, especially those who work with the deaf or hard-of-hearing. The San Francisco SPCA Hearing Dog Program selects what they call "signaling" dogs, but they might also be selecting excellent "signing" dogs. (In the book *Lend Me an Ear*, Martha Hoffman explains the selection and training of the signaling dog.) Though the signaling dogs at the SF/SPCA communicate differently than our signing dogs, happy, high-energy, attentive dogs are excellent candidates for both alerting and signing. The signaling dog alerts by drawing attention, and bringing the person, to the issue. The signing dog can alert but might also be able to specifically communicate with K9Signs. Some alerts that could be specifically communicated through sign are **Fire, Alarm, Door, Siren, Car,** and **People's Names.**

Beyond alerting, the K9Signer communicates for nonalerting purposes. For a dog that already signals, learning K9Sign or K9*ASL* should be fun. K9*ASL* hearing dogs paired with people using American Sign Language would communicate well, in both directions, as each would use either the original or modified form of American Sign Language.

As different professional and personal uses of signing are developed, customized versions of AnimalSign will evolve. A dedicated search and rescue (SAR) dog will need different signs than an alerting dog. I am currently elaborating a custom version for SAR dogs, dogs assisting the blind, and other service and assistance dog categories. Companion animals (especially with human partners with lots of time) can pick and choose gestures after learning the basics of the language for home and play use. The basic and intermediate signs of K9Sign Language build the foundation for language learning. With this foundation, dogs can continue their language education.

I encourage you to try teaching language to other animals—rats, birds, cats, goats, cows, elephants. Observe what they do with it. My cats were not enthusiastic about signing initially, but over time AngelFur and Pastel have become interested in this and other forms of communicating, which I am developing for them. Elephants would need a customized Gestuary to make use of their magnificent flexible trunk.

LEARNING SEQUENCE

AnimalSign Language learning is structured as a set of sequential lessons. You begin by learning the prerequisite skills which include training obedience, and how to provide feedback and reinforcements, which are detailed in the upcoming chapters. Next, you will need to learn the Human K9Signs that your dog must learn to understand, but will not sign to you. These Human K9Signs include your feedback, statements, requests, and questions addressed to your dog. Once you have mastered the Human K9Signs, you can learn how to teach your dog her own signs, listed in the Canine K9Sign Gestuary. The Basic/Foundation signs in the Canine K9Sign Gestuary are simple, fun, and easy to learn. These initial signs motivate your dog to learn other signs. The Intermediate signs take more schooling, but are useful and engaging. The Advanced signs teach names that are important to your dog. If you want to use just a few signs with your dog, then learn the Basic/Foundation and pick from the Intermediate signs. But if you want your dog to potentially learn language as a lifetime skill, you will need to learn all the signs.

Learning the signs as a potential lifetime language will provide you and your dog with powerful tools to communicate. Your dog may even begin to combine signs—to create sentences. Just as children need to learn the alphabet in order to make words, and words are needed to create new sentences, your dog needs to learn the signing basics in order to use them as a language for more elaborate communication. Signing empowers dogs to actively, visibly expand communication—in a way that we humans can recognize and respond to!

The Benefits

AnimalSign Language has both theoretical and practical benefits. Theoretically, teaching animals to use a sign language will expose various aspects of their cognition, especially animal language capability. Currently the language structure reflects human (my) thinking patterns; nonetheless we can still gather much information about animal's thinking patterns. I and other signers have seen and documented dogs and horses learning and using these new gestures and signs, as well as creating and combining their own gestures them for what appears to be simple communication. Chal and other signers learn to gesture, or even sign, to name or ask for *Food, Chicken, Liver Water, Toy, Ball, Door, Phone, Sean, Debbie,* and *Pick Up.* Both dog and horse signers have spontaneously communicated combination of signs, taught individually (*Colored Bucket* and *Sean, Chicken* and *Play Name, Chicken, Class*). Chal has created her own signs seeming to ask for *Help* and *Show Me.* Chal has signed *Food* directly to a fly, perhaps suggesting interspecies communication. A poodle used the food sign to indicate *Water* before learning the sign for *Water.*

With continued AnimalSign Language education, can and will these signers expand this signing into complex communication and true language? Years of study might reveal the answer. We can better understand how and what animals communicate and the intricacies of their perceptual world. We can find out what their language process is, and how different and similar it is to ours. We can delve into what kind of thoughts they have and how they structure these into communications. Regardless of the particular answers, we can pose new cognitive questions, ones not yet imagined.

The practice of animals using a sign language to communicate to humans and other animals has limitless uses. Some of what humans and animals perceive can be mapped to words. When these words are communicated, they can enrich the human-animal bond. This skill can improve animals' lives by enabling them to ask for what they need, express themselves, and thus reduce frustration. For rescue animals, signing speeds up the processes of bonding and trusting. For working (assistance, alerting, rescue, etc.) dogs, the ability to specifically communicate what they sense improves their confidence, performance, value, and perhaps their self-esteem.

What It Is Not

AnimalSign and its sublanguages are not the natural body languages of animals, though natural gestures may be used and assigned specific meanings in AnimalSign. The gestures are not finger spelling or American Sign Language. While AnimalSign Languages are logical and intuitive, they do not rely on nonvisible communication (though a person or animal may use intuition to aid the communication, teaching, and learning process.) Teachers (of human students) who combine intuition with their teaching methods have been found to be effective educators. Whatever it takes, use it!

Learning and teaching AnimalSign Languages are not quick processes; they take time and effort. But by following the plan laid out in this book, progress can be swift. The beginning signs, which are based on natural, frequently made moves, may be learned quickly. Learning more intermediate and advanced moves takes more time. Learning to associate a meaning, or outcome, with a gesture takes even longer. Grasping the symbolic nature of the communication concepts, if even occurring, would require more fruitful engagement and observation. As naturally adept toward learning language as humans are, teaching them the rules and subtleties of language takes years. Humans have fewer than twenty years to solidify language (and up to one hundred years to expand it). Teaching dogs or horses language has to happen faster. Some dogs can live around fifteen years and companion horses around thirty years. Elephants who live to be over one hundred years would have time for many lessons! We don't know the span of the critical period for animal language development, but we would expect it to begin early in life, as it does in humans.

Some animal students may experience delays in observable learning, others may pick up quickly, then plateau. This plateau can occur at various times during the learning process. One particular plateau is noted as a prelearning dip (see Karen Pryor's and Diane Bauman's books on animal training for further information). Many factors play into how well an animal learns a gesture. Animal genes, physique, cognition (especially intelligence type and level), teacher skills, teaching methods, and language structure are all important factors. Some are well studied, others are in need of research. Teaching language to nonprimate animals is a new field—with everything to discover and enjoy.

My own experimenting with Chal revealed many delays and confusions that required my backing up and rerouting education efforts. Chal learned the food sign easily. But it took her a while to offer the food gesture herself. Lifting the left paw for food was easy, but lifting the right for toy was more difficult—she wanted to use her left. (Was she left pawed?) After learning each sign, we practiced comparing *Toy* and *Food* in the same session. That comparison was very helpful. A miniature poodle I worked with already knew some tricks and learned these first two gestures quickly. Chal, with her own inclinations and temperament, takes her time learning. After getting a sign correct in one session, Chal will immediately get it wrong in the next, then with more practice gets it right. Her process is repeated with each sign. But once she learns, she has it. Chal also uses her new gestures creatively, and makes up her own while we interact.

AnimalSign teaching is not obedience training. Teaching language is both similar to, and different from, teaching obedience. They are similar in that both involve learning and require objectives, teaching, practice, proofing, patience, and time. Both make use of operant conditioning—conditioning a voluntary response (gesture) as a learning method. But teaching language to animals requires more patience and time than obedience training. It requires discrimination training and a special allowance for creativity from the animal, as it asks her for spontaneous and thoughtful behavior, and generally not for obedience. (Though telling an animal to sign is asking her to obey in a communicative way.) Animals, especially at early stages of learning, must be allowed to initiate communication, to make requests without prompting or obtaining permission from the teacher. The obedience perspective of language learning comes in the form of demanding a behavior and making corrections as needed to assure compliance. The language teaching perspective is to look for communications and signs, encourage attempts to sign, and to assist, bring out, even give cues to assist learning. Many trainers and scientists have explored teaching methods that promote creativity, such as trial-and-error and shaping as well as rewarding creativity itself.

An animal with just obedience training will have specific challenges to overcome when first learning to sign. The animal may be reluctant to do something without being told, perhaps fearing a mistake (and the punishment that may follow). So, during obedience training, never use the negative **No** with your dog. Instead use the more encouraging sound **Na,** suggesting "not this way, darling; keep trying." Obedience training and language education should not be taught in the same session, especially if any punishment or "compulsion" is used with the former.

AnimalSign Language is not just training your dog to perform trivial tricks. But whether animals learn tricks, or tricks associated with meanings, or AnimalSigns, they all expand an animal's cognitive repertoire. Simple tricks can be entertaining. Just as gestures that are used symbolically become language, infusing tricks with meaning ("meaving") creatively transforms tricks into words—language. This level of communication could be useful in many animal professions. Linking cued tricks to meaningful words connects a gesture to language. For example, instead of a teaching a dog to count in response to a cue (from the trainer or audience), teaching a dog to *really* count involves some language lessons. Teaching a dog to subtract two numbers would provide a mechanism to teach syntax (where order matters). Instead of teaching a dog to nod in response to a nod cue, teaching a dog to nod when she might mean **Yes!** links a trick to a real meaning, a real word **Yes!** Expanding our perception and expectations of animals allows us to take a more receptive and objective look at what our animals are capable of. Appreciating our animals' skills and abilities, especially for potential language, is beneficial to our relationships. An animal's ability to understand (by various means) and communicate with her natural body language is truly amazing. But for dogs in particular that are so immersed in our human society, their natural but limited communication makes them seem illiterate and undereducated. They have the potential for so much more communication.

CHAPTER 3

Understanding How Dogs Learn

Humans and animals can learn. It is both hard- and softwired into our brains. Each individual creature has its own learning inclinations, talents, and styles. Training animals to learn and perform tasks on command, to modify their behavior, and to think independently has been studied and documented. More recent works have adapted the knowledge of human behavior and learning for use with animals, and vice versa.

The Science of Learning

The science of learning pools information, models, and techniques from many fields. Relevant fields include ethology (especially cognitive), psychology (especially cognitive and behavioral), physiology (especially neurophysiology), animal and human development, linguistics, and practical fields of human education and animal training. I have integrated elements from these fields to formulate the animal language lesson plans in this book.

Observation (using all senses) is critical to any science. The field of ethology focuses on observing and documenting natural behavior. Ethology studies observable behavior (an effect) that is enticed (caused) by sources and events. Physiological and psychological drives play a role in producing behaviors. This field aims to separate the cause of an observed behavior, from the presumed or interpreted feelings and emotions that humans tend to associate with a cause of a behavior. Take this example: A dog is eating and you take away her food. It stands upright with ears forward and up, muzzle wrinkled, canines showing, and growling. The ethological observations focus on those physical observations of the dog's behavior—the "effects." These were "caused" by a physical event—you took away the food. The cognitive events occur inside the dog's mind are not observable (yet), so you only guess at what could be happening. Because it isn't always possible to make strict, ethnological extrapolations in daily life, you may take liberties that extend beyond that scientific view and elaborate that the dog may be angry and trying to get back at you for taking the food. (This might be a useful anthropomorphic interpretation for you to process and learn from, for your future interactions with your dog and her food.)

Observation as a tool is very useful, especially for research and teaching. But, as I've just explained, it has its limits. It is not purely objective. Any observer will focus on and perceive target objects attended to, and block out some other information. Our attention limits our observations to the intended objective. If you were at a party and someone you were attracted to walked in, your attention would focus on them, and you would ignore other people and events at the party. Much is blocked out. One way to get around this limit is to deliberately reobserve similar situations with different perspectives and goals.

In the following examples, take note of your different observations from each of the events. For each, write down who you observe to be the important players, what the important events are, and what is going on.

- Be a dog handler and observe a dog greeting another dog.
- Be an observer and have someone else (a trainer) handle the dog in the same situation.
- As an observer, imagine the dogs are genius humans.
- As an observer, imagine the two dogs are very simple creatures.
- As an observer, imagine the dogs as machines or robots.
- Imagine yourself as one of the dogs.

For each scenario, write down all your observations and reflect on what you focused on and what you ignored. Then examine the attitude and expectations you had in each scenario. Your senses, state of mind, attention, and goals affect your observations, perceptions, and interpretations of the world around you.

Physiology, psychology, and developmental fields have many contributions to understanding learning. The function of anatomical body parts is critical to any learning and memory attempt. Without the intact neuroanatomy and nervous system, learning and memory will not occur. The anatomical development of the known maturing animal systems is somewhat understood. We need more information, and much research is going on, to better understand where and how higher levels of learning (beyond stimulus-response) anatomically occur and respond. A stimulus (food) will cause a response (salivating) in animals. In humans, a stimulus tap on the knee will cause a (spinal cord reflex) response of the lower leg jerking out. Your doctor might have demonstrated this during an exam. Higher levels of learning involve integrated brain activities. Although research has shown planning, anticipating, and organizing involves the frontal lobe (the front part of the brain), much is left to uncover about the numerous higher-levels of cognition. Psychology has made advances in the understanding of learning needs, processes, and outcomes through several experimentations on stimulus enticed, command-based, and procedural learning, especially in animals. Attention and motivation, critical to learning, is also studied.

The practical fields of human education and animal training contain much information for human and animal language students. Methods of teaching human students appear more general than those used with animals. For humans, we are encouraged to teach (often to groups) by modeling (with students observing and imitating), combined with some shaping and discovery methods, followed by practice and reinforcement. With humans, we teach procedures and strategies for independent learning. With animals, we teach (often individually) procedural tasks, using operant conditioning—that is, using rewards or punishment to change their behavior. We use a variety of very specific techniques, timed appropriately. The animal training field is filled with books, many with insightful perspectives, methods, and tips, but others with old, inefficient methods. Some more advanced dog training methods teach problem solving and alerting. The ability of animals to learn by observation (and then imitate) in most research has not been repeatedly demonstrated in adult dogs. But I have seen dogs and horses imitate and learn how to learn by observation. Some studies have shown theses animals learn well by vocal command and instruction. So we need to teach how to **Copy** and **Don't Copy** us, then put it into practice. Whenever we claim our animals don't know or can't do something, we should try to *teach* that something, then re-evaluate. I put this into practice in AnimalSign by teaching **Copy** and **Don't Copy** as well as *Try* to my human and animal students.

Chal can imitate movements and will be tested on how she can use a newly learned move for problem solving. Some of my human students in mathematics needed to be taught how to extend their learning by imitation into more creative problem solving. The key was to convince them that what I was teaching was not the only way to do a problem. I accomplished this task by leaving a problem mostly unsolved and up to them to resolve. While training dogs to problem solve rather than showing them how to solve the problem, it is more productive to allow them to find alterative solutions to achieve the same goal.

Linguistics, the study of language, helps us understand the development and use of language (as we define it). We know about the building blocks of language, the various forms, the required developmental anatomy, and the learning stages in some mammals, primates, and some birds. We know possible meanings of some natural body language in primates, sea mammals, dogs, cats, horses, birds, and others. Learned, productive language has been intensely studied in humans, and we have many languages to compare— oral, written, and signed. A few language-trained parrots have been studied for years. But *learned* productive language capability in dogs and horses is new and now being studied at the AnimalSign Center.

Learning Principles

Learning and behavior-modifying strategies are based on a few key principles. Though each animal (mammalian) species has particular inclinations, the underlying simple mechanisms for particular types of learning appear to be similar. Learning has been extensively studied and documented for certain types of behavior. Two ways to classify learning are procedural and conceptual. Procedural learning is how to do something (move left leg up). Conceptual learning involves ideas, such as making connections (associations) between events (sit and a treat appears) or understanding the goal of a command. The learned meaning of an animal's gestures may reflect conceptual learning.

Key concepts that explain some learning are classical and operant conditioning. Grasping these concepts requires understanding the meaning and use of reinforcement, punishment, and feedback. Punishment concepts help us understand behavior, but I don't use them while teaching language. Studies have shown that punishment (something perceived as unwanted) tends to decrease an animal's (including a human's) performance of a behavior. Mild repeated punishment generally isn't effective, as it becomes "nagging" which can be ignored. Punishment can be mild, as when you take away your favorite shoe that your dog is chewing, or it can be a tug on the leash, to keep your dog with you. Researchers have learned from punishment how an animal responds. For language work, it is not needed and will tarnish the whole process. For detailed explanations of the key ideas, refer to *How Dogs Learn* by Mary R. Burch and Jon S. Bailey, and *Handbook of Applied Dog Behavior and Training* by Steven R. Lindsay.

Simple learning mechanisms for voluntary behavior in the dog, horse, and human involve operant conditioning. The ease of learning differs for each act and species as well as each individual. Every animal has different learning tendencies and abilities, as these enable survival. Each species has different places in evolution and the food chain, genetic makeup, environment and living conditions, training methods used, and learning styles. All these and many other factors impact various aspects of learning.

Understanding these ideas and when and how to apply them will strengthen your ability to teach your dog language. As you apply the knowledge to your own animals, start simply and use what works. I integrate useful concepts and techniques from human teaching and animal training for teaching language to animals.

Language training occurs through operant conditioning and association. Operant conditioning is built on the idea that the consequences of a voluntary behavior determine future behavior. A positive consequence (a reward) that follows an animal's behavior increases the animal's repetition of that behavior. Makes sense—"sit gets treat, then more sit equals more treat." The positive consequence reinforces the behavior. If the consequence for a behavior is unpleasant, the animal will perform that behavior less often. "Pulling leash gets collar jerk, no pulling means no collar jerk." Learning occurs when the animal connects the behavior with the consequence. But when the animal actually modifies her behavior further, another step in learning has occurred. She has decided to act on her conceptual learning to modify her behavior to gain more control of what she wants. I was teaching Chal how to position herself on my left side, facing forward, from any location she was originally. When she was in front facing me, with me still, I moved the leash counterclockwise, to my left around to the back and forward, so that she would end up facing forward by my left side. Chal, being rather large, had a hard time making such a tight circle (at my left side). On her own she understood the goal and spontaneously, from in front of me, went around my right side, behind me, then appeared head first on my left side. Chal used conceptual understanding and learning when she understood a goal (that I failed to achieve with her using my process), and she found her solution to it rather than obeying the procedural solution I was trying to teach her. (As we all know, the animal may know what we want her to do, but decide that is not what she wants at that time.) Animal brains (humans included) are wired to learn, to make connections.

Another key idea in learning theory is classical conditioning. This refers to training an *involuntary* body response to occur after a new stimulus or cue. A cue can elicit either an involuntary or voluntary response. If the response is involuntary, then the response is considered to be achieved through classical conditioning; if it is voluntary, this is achieved through operant conditioning. An example of classical conditioning is when the sound of the food can opening (new cue) results in a dog involuntarily salivating (response). An example of operant conditioning is when the sound of the food can being opened results in a dog learning to voluntarily respond by sitting.

Some of my clients ask about teaching a specific sign to indicate the need to **Potty, Poop,** or **Pee.** In K9Sign, these are learned gestures mapped to internal natural urges and wanted actions. Taking an anthropomorphic approach, we assume a dog's desire to, and control of a, **Potty** is much like ours. We can presume our dogs feel the same as we do. We can have some animal empathy.

Teaching to **Potty** on request involves both involuntary and voluntary mechanisms. The desire initially appears involuntarily but the control (when and where to allow a **Potty**) occurs voluntarily. The reason we can learn to control this activity is based on the physiology and anatomy of the muscles and nerves involved. We have a voluntary muscle at the very end of our digestive system allowing us to control defecation. Without this voluntarily controlled muscle, dogs would not be able to allow or stop a **Poop.** We can prompt the original, involuntary desire to **Poop,** and we can help voluntarily control when and where to **Poop.** Learning to voluntarily gesture **Potty** or **Poop** to indicate the presence of this feeling (and the desire to end this feeling) is taught through conditioning. If learning has to do with the involuntary movements from reflexes (such as defecating), we refer to these as classical conditioning. Most of the signs in this book are voluntary responses and thus are (in part) taught with operant conditioning. Other processes are also used to teach signs, such as imitation.

Motivating an animal to learn new things is very important and involves reinforcers—rewards. The innate rewards are primary reinforcers such as food or comfort. You can teach a dog to consider other things as reinforcers (such as **Yes!** with the clicker sound, petting, or a head nod) through conditioning. You can do this by teaching your dog to associate (expect) a reward with conditioned reinforcers. To create a conditioned reinforcer, present the secondary reinforcer (**Yes!** and/or a click) before the primary reinforcer (food). This conditions your dog to accept the **Yes!** (and/or the click) itself as the learned reward; expecting food will often follow.

Clapping, sounding delighted, praising, clicking, **Yes!**, and many other actions and sounds, gestures, objects, or outcomes can become conditioned reinforcers. Saying **Yes!** and clicking work especially well together. Some natural situations present their own innate rewards. The animal pushes a door, the door opens, animal goes into the food room. The behavior is push, the reward is the animal gets to go in the desired room to have access to the food. If a dog offers the **Potty** gesture, the reward is you open the door and let her go out to potty.

Teaching a naturally occurring behavior to occur on cue is easy. Imagine you want to teach your dog to fetch and bring back a ball. One part of this is to teach your dog to bite a ball (unlike Labs, not all dogs are "natural" retrievers or even enjoy doing this). You can wait for the behavior to occur and give the cue words or sign (***Bite***). After the behavior is performed, give the feedback (***Yes!***) and reward (let your dog keep and play with ball itself). The "trick" is in setting up a situation where the animal will more likely offer the behavior, then you can label the behavior and reward the dog. You can use guided feedback to help steer the move while it is in progress.

To combine a series of behaviors into one labeled gesture (fetch the ball), you'd use the method of shaping by chain the smaller behaviors: get the ball, bring the ball from the living room, drop it here. For other gestures, you may need to physically mold/move the dog's body or prompt her to imitate you (or a picture or stuffed animal). Whatever the method, it is up to us, the teachers, to make it worthwhile for our animal students to learn how to gesture. The more that gesturing enables an animal to control and predict its environment, the more motivated and receptive the animal will be to learning gesturing.

Applying learning theory to teaching language involves instructing in two stages. The first stage is to teach a move, then put it under cue control. The cue can be a sound or move you make. Most training methods focus on using cues to control a behavior or a response, and thus many techniques are available to teach an animal to move. Learning moves is like learning tricks, devoid of innate meaning other than implying a reward.

The second stage is to teach the connection between a learned move and a specific meaning. There are two approaches here. For easy moves, you may opt to teach the move and meaning together, as in ***Food.*** The other sure approach for any sign, including ones with difficult or rarely gestured moves, you teach the move first, get it on cue, then teach the meaning. Teaching the sign ***Phone*** is a good example.

For signs that have easy or commonly gestured moves, a quick method is to teach the move and its meaning together. This is useful for some words—***Food***—these two stages (movement and meaning) can be learned together As you manually mold your dog's body into the move—or she makes the move on her own—you sign/say the word, then show the meaning. Over time your dog learns to connect, to associate, the move with the meaning. This is due to the fact that food is the name of the object and the reward, so dogs grasp the meaning right away. They easily associate moving their front leg with your giving a treat. Not all signs are this obvious.

To teach a more difficult sign, such as *Phone,* you'd teach the move, get it on cue, then teach the meaning. Here you would teach the move (right paw scraping the side of the face and down), get the move on cue (*Sign Phone*), then teach the meaning by having the phone present and visible.

Teaching a move's meaning can happen in phases itself. Initially, to the dog, the meaning is the consequence of the gesture—the reward. After fading (gradually not providing) the reward, the consequence can become the gesture's meaning. The meaning of the consequence also changes. At first, the meaning is that the gesture points to the consequence. Later the gesture may come to mean, to represent, the consequence. The more useful the gesture, the more effective this transition. A good example of this occurs when teaching the meaning of *Water.* (Since we are dealing with meaning, let's presume the dog already knows the move, and you can cue the move by signing/saying *Sign Water.*) Initially when you cue your dog to *Sign Water,* you then present the water and a treat. The dog will learn when she signs, water appears, followed by a motivational treat. The dog may also learn that when water is present and she signs *Water,* she gets a treat. She knows how to get a treat, she signs *Water,* when she is cued or when water is present. With practice in real situations, such as teaching meaning when a dog is thirsty, eventually we maximize the possibility she will learn the meaning of her *Water* sign. When your dog has a connection between the sign and water, you can stop dropping a treat in the water. Water is reward enough.

Entice your dog to sign *Water* and provide the consequence (water) and an added reward—a wet treat, such as jerky dipped in water. Initially the meaning is the consequence, the treat reward. After enticing her to sign *Water* several times, you fade the wet treat reward, occasionally giving the wet treat. Finally you give only the changed meaning of the consequence, the water itself. Eventually we aim to have the dog attach the meaning (not as a consequence) alone to the sign.

The difference between traditional training and language teaching is that with language teaching you don't have to cue the animal to sign to you. The animal provides the gesture on her own when she wants to. Say a dog learns a move, lifting its left paw up, then down. The move's name is *Food.* The dog learns the move's meaning when she anticipates the food, which appears after she makes the move. (Now the move has become a gesture.) Next, the dog associates the gesture. *Food* as a way to indicate (its desire or knowledge of) food. Language learning has occurred when the dog uses the sign *Food* not only as a way to make food arrive but also as a symbolic representation of food itself, perhaps to tell you something about the food itself. Studying this possible symbolic transition is fascinating and challenging. Ingenious tests need to be used to capture this transition, should it occur.

Understanding learning theory provides you with a basis to teach language. You will use various techniques described in this book (some techniques also described in the referenced literature) to teach moves and meanings. These include shaping, free shaping, trial and error, luring, prompting, molding, modeling, imitation, and direct instruction. You will use feedback tools such as *Yes!*, guided feedback, and the clicker to convey to your dog how close she is to doing what you want (and getting what she wants). When you have the move under cue control, you teach the move's meaning.

Teaching meaning can occur in various ways, one is priming the meaning, then teaching in one or two directions. (Earlier I discussed ways to teach the sign by teaching the move and meaning separately or together. This section deals with two directions of teaching the *meaning* of the sign.) Priming is where you expose your dog to the word and/or sign for a concept, by saying/signing *IS Word* as you point to something. As you hold a toy, you'd say *IS Toy*. This uses receptive language. One direction of teaching meaning would occur when you cue your dog (*Sign Toy*), or your dog signs *Toy* on her own, then you make the toy appear. Your dog moves, you provide the meaning—*Toy*. The second direction of teaching meaning is when you present the toy and then cue your dog to sign *Toy*. You need to be consistent and well trained as she learns meanings. (Your reward is the pleasure of controlling your dog's learning—good teacher you!)

Literature

Several excellent books and journals document and explain what we know about learning, teaching, and training in dogs and other animals. Many focus on the ideas and methods needed to train animals to perform and obey various commands. Some focus on teaching animals to think, to alert, and to behave creatively. Other books summarize our current knowledge of animal learning and training.

The Other End of the Leash by Patricia McConnell explains some differences in animal and human inclinations and communication. It examines the human-dog relationship and how interspecies understanding impacts training effectiveness. *The Culture Clash* by Jean Donaldson explains this cultural difference between human and animal behavioral expectations, elaborates on training principles, and gives many real-life examples.

How Dogs Learn by Mary Burch and Jon Bailey provides an academic view of learning and training principles, along with explanations of behavior and training theories, and a summary review of key principles. Clarence Pfaffenberger's aptly titled *The New Knowledge of Dog Behavior* offers insights to the working dog. *Beyond Basic Dog Training* by Diane Bauman focuses on teaching rather than training dogs and on methods of teaching dogs to think. The book also explains and diagrams the basic training moves. One very clear, easy-to-read reference is *The Everything Dog Training and Tricks Book* by Gerilyn Bielakiewicz. It is well organized, clearly explained—a great refresher. For puppy training, I highly recommend Ian Dunbar's work on positive puppy training *Before and After Getting Your Puppy.*

Karen Pryor's groundbreaking *Don't Shoot the Dog!* explains the basis of learning and conditioning, as well as useful tools (such as the clicker) that facilitate and enhance communication during training with your dog. This book brought updated, scientifically based animal training methods to the dog-training world.

For an understanding of dog body language, refer to the outstanding and well-organized book by Roger Abrantes called *Dog Language.* Brenda Aloff's book *Canine Body Language: A Photographic Guide Interpreting the Native Language of the Domestic Dog* offers a visual guide to canine body language. Both *The Intelligence of Dogs* by Stanley Coren and Bruce Fogle's *The Dog's Mind* provide a solid understanding of what we know about dog cognition. Other titles on this subject that you will want to read are *If Your Dog Could Talk* by Bruce Fogle, *If Dogs Could Talk* by Vilmos Csanyi, and *On Talking Terms with Dogs* by Turid Rurgaas. If you are interested learning how to evaluate the intelligence of your puppy view, Dr. Laura Pasten's video on *How Smart Is Your Puppy?* For an in-depth examination of the literature and knowledge of adaptation and learning in dogs, refer to the *Handbook of Applied Dog Behavior and Training* by Stephen R. Lindsay. For a recent overview of behavior, cognition, and evolution, examine Adam Miklosi's *Dog Behavior, Evolution, and Cognition.*

Rupert Sheldrake writes about fascinating animal perceptions in *Dogs That Know When Their Owners Are Coming Home.* In *Animal Bodies, Human Minds*, W. A. Hillix and Duane Rumbaugh discuss the documented existence of a dog named Fellow around the year 1924, who responded to two hundred English words. In *Science* (June 2004), Juliane Kaminski and others document the studies (and Paul Bloom comments) on a dog named Rico. Rico was tested and found to recognize two hundred German words spoken to him by his owner. This documentation has sparked a long-overdue interest in canine cognition, with the focus on understanding language. We now see an increased interest in scientifically based canine biology and cognition studies. The very first Canine Science Forum took place in Hungary in 2008, aiding the establishment of canine biology as an interdisciplinary field of science.

Despite many books on the subject, academically we know relatively little about canine cognition. Much is written about conditioning and command-based training and skill, some about learning and natural productive language, little about receptive language, and virtually nothing about thought processes, learned productive language, or other higher-cognitive capabilities. Some knowledge is anecdotal or undocumented, privately observed in the homes of animal caretakers and enthusiasts. People teach, or their pets display, remarkable skills. New research that examines problem-solving skills, and other intelligent canine behaviors is beginning to surface. A dog's ability to categorize visual images on special cards, language boards, or computer screens by touching can now be tested. One value of the computer is that social cues affecting results are no longer an issue. People do not need to be near the dog to test a response, thus visual cueing is not present. With computers, the ability of dogs to recall their owner's face after hearing the voice can be studied.

Despite many new studies and all the literature that is currently available, much folklore and myth remain on how animals think and learn, and what they can and can't do. Many trainers have practical and useful tips—though their explanation of the reasons for learning may not be scientifically supported. Myths about reinforcement and punishment are widespread. In training, the animal's perception of liking or disliking something is key. One misguided technique (found in horse training) is to stop the training as soon as the horse does what you want. But this technique is only effective if the animal doesn't like doing what you ask. If she dislikes what you are asking her to do, she will perceive stopping as a reward for doing what you ask. However, if she likes what you're asking her to do, she will perceive stopping as a negative, a punishment. This is true for all animals. What would you (being an anthropomorphic animal) think of having to stop something you like once you do it right? Mind twisted, you might think it better to delay doing what was asked so that you may keep *almost* doing what you like—longer. (Let the games begin!)

Some trainers believe animals are only creatures of habit—that they don't think. For animal experts and scientists, the definition of "think" differs with different animals and trainers. But we do have evidence suggesting animals think, and process perceptions and actions. Friederike Range has demonstrated that we now can place dogs in front of touch-screen computers and present image choices (for them to tap) to examine their thinking and reasoning. The person testing does not need to know the question nor answer, which minimizes influencing the dogs' reaction. With technology such as EEGs, PET, and MRI scans adapted for animal cognition studies, more evidence will become available to show the details of thinking in animals. Some simple thinking and reasoning can be tested through rule-based computer programs. Animals can follow rules. In fact, many are excellent with simple rules, and expect *us* to follow them better. The challenge is to teach more sophisticated rules to them.

As I've mentioned, some experts and laypeople have ruled out that dogs could have cognitive abilities, such as language, that are similar to ours. But we haven't yet explored how our language and communication is similar to or different from theirs. Dogs are mammals, as we are, with some similar brain anatomy; thus we should expect some similarities in cognitive brain function. We don't have adequate information to exclude the possibility of a language potential in these animals. We need to study it first. We tend to see what we look for and not see what we don't expect. We get back what we teach. If we haven't taught a formal productive language to animals, it's no wonder if they don't produce it. Studying the potential for canine productive (gestural) language is a wide-open field. K9Sign is dedicated to this mapping.

Language Research

Before discussing the research on animals taught to sign, I will discuss the far more sophisticated human language and research. Much research exists on teaching gestures, signs, and gestural language to humans. We have learned some very interesting facts about human language processing from this. Often the humans studied are deaf or hard-of-hearing. Now many hearing people have the wonderful opportunity to learn the beautiful American Sign Language (ASL), or other signed languages, as second or third languages. Fortunately courses in ASL have become an option in some secondary schools. At one time, linguists did not consider ASL a legitimate, formal language. Later, with more research, it was shown to be a true language, using many of the same regions of the brain as oral or written languages. ASL requires, and uses, some of the same essential brain areas as the oral and written languages. When deaf people who sign have strokes involving the brain language centers, they cannot sign in language form anymore—though they can make simple gestures and pantomime. For a rich, fascinating academic look at sign language research and cognition, read Karen Emmorey's book on *Language, Cognition, and the Brain.* For several articles, videos, books and products for babies learning to sign, see Linda Acredolo's Baby Signs website.

From the existing research on babies learning to sign with simple gestures, we might wonder whether babies learning the simple language Baby Signs might develop the language areas of their brains. Long-term follow-up studies are possible with these babies. Over many years, if dogs did appear to learn and use AnimalSign Language, then we would need to examine what regions of their brains were stimulated. Would they be stimulating the complex or simple language center, or something else? If dogs used AnimalSign Language but it didn't seem clear that they were doing so as a language, we would still want to know what brain regions they were using for whatever they were doing with it. Whether the essential areas of the brain in animals that have learned AnimalSign Language are stimulated and even changed in a similar way to humans will take many years to assess.

As more data are gathered by animal language learners of varying breeds and ages, we will have a better linguistic understanding of animal communication, and a better understanding of the potential for nonprimate animals to learn productive language. With multiple pups per litter, not too many years apart, very interesting studies with controls can occur. I wonder if the brain's language center of a dog learning K9Sign Language will differ from a "twin" who didn't learn it. Will learning K9Sign significantly change the signing pup's brain as she grows? We are in an exciting time, a new era with intense focus on studying the cognition, intelligence, and language potential of various animals. Much of the research on canines centers on the natural body and receptive language. Some literature examines canine natural productive body and vocal language, but very little exists on learned, productive gestural canine language. This is the mission of the AnimalSign Center.

Today dogs are entering new and highly specialized professions. Some specialties require dogs to sense something and alert (gesture) accordingly, as in hearing/signaling dogs. In others, the dog is taught to "read" a sign or a stylized picture and respond with the appropriate behavior. Dogs are taught to search for and rescue living people, or search for and recover dead bodies. Dogs are taught to alert to various sounds and smells such as oils, plastics, termites, and even cancer cells.

Much research already exists on canine learning. A few researchers provide interesting studies of receptive language. At AnimalSign Center, we focus on developing ways of enhancing a canine's ability to communicate. One method is by teaching dogs K9Sign or K9*ASL*—learned productive languages. Dogs are already using the K9Sign Language to ask for different food types and water, different toy types, stating they need to go potty, or get picked up, as well as naming specific people and objects. With these animal language tools, I can envision a future where dogs and other animals might sign learned and natural words, forming sentences with their bodies, as they convey the details of their perceptions. This will greatly expand human-animal communication, relationship, and service. These might just teach *us* a word or two about their world, their cognition, and our own language.

CHAPTER 4

Learning K9Sign

Attempting to teach a dog to use gestures as language requires preparation. A prerequisite your dog needs is basic obedience. She must be able to obey sit, stand, down, stay, come, and look (at you). To teach signs, your dog must also accept your handling all her body parts.

K9Sign Language lessons are organized into Human and Canine K9Signs. You sign the Human K9Signs and your dog signs the Canine K9Signs. You will need to learn all the Human Signs as they are essential to teaching any Canine Signs. The Canine K9Signs are organized into levels: Basic/Foundation, Intermediate, and Advanced. This book covers all the Human K9Signs and all the Basic/Foundation, several Intermediate, and a few Advanced level Canine K9Signs. These will pave the road to expanding communication with signs, into language. Many more Canine K9Signs will be available to learn in future resources.

While providing your canine with language education, you'll be learning and teaching gestures using various tools that have previously been shown to be effective with both humans and animals. The focus in this book is on the alphabet (beginning language building) signs and on language tools that are easy, essential, and practical. This simplicity ensures positive experiences and enables the building of solid skills for future language development. Though you will be signing Human K9Signs, your pet must learn to understand your new gestures and behave accordingly, but your pet need not gesture herself. Some Basic canine signs take advantage of moves dogs naturally offer. These signs represent simple and concrete objects and concepts that dogs clearly understand, such as play, food, and toy.

Tools/Strategies

You'll need tools and strategies to steer your dog's behaviors toward the correct responses. Some tools you will use are guided feedback (**Yah, Yeah, Yes!**), inspiring moves, and cueing the moves (now tricks) with your request to communicate (**Sign**), useful commands (**Attend**), and various methods to inspire moves, and associate moves with meanings. Giving feedback, requesting attention, and signing are important and used for all signs. If you know how to teach your dog tricks and she already performs them, you'll already have a head start teaching her the move for a sign—that will be a trick. With the trick (the move under cue), you'll be able jump ahead and simply learn how, and teach her, to assign meaning to those tricks.

Guided feedback provides your dog with information about how close she is to gesturing correctly. This step-by-step feedback gives more information than the simple **Yes!** or **No** verbal response from you, which you would use when your dog doesn't have to stop and learn steps on the way, but will keep trying until you say **Yes!** Guided feedback provides several levels of information, from **Na** (*Not that*) to **Yah** (*Close*) to **Yeah** (*Almost*) to **Yes!** (*Got it*).

This feedback is extremely effective and efficient. If you and your dogs already use a good feedback mechanism, try the guided approach as well and then use what works best for your dog.

The following is an example of how to use guided feedback to help your dog find a hidden treat. Throw a treat in a field, and ask your dog to fetch it. When your dog goes in the wrong direction, say and gesture **Na** to indicate that she's going the wrong way. As your dog gets closer to the treat, say and sign **Yah** to let her know she's close to it; **Yeah** means very close; and finally, **Yes!** means right there—you got it.

Several strategies are embedded in each lesson to facilitate learning. The overall procedure for teaching your dog to learn is as follows:

1. Activate receptive language by talking to your dog, and listening and watching what she communicates.

2. Prime your dog for word learning using *IS* as you label objects.

3. Learn and teach the Human K9Signs.

4. Teach the Canine K9Signs in the order presented.

5. Journal (and review) your experiences.

Initially dogs need to learn language step-by-step. Just as with traditional training: first your dog learns obedience, then moves on to other training, such as agility, and tracking. Just as with humans: first we learn the alphabet, then we learn to read. Follow this guide. Don't skip steps, you might trip. Throughout each phase, make signing fun.

Stages

As you learn and experiment with the formal lessons, you and your dog will pass through learning phases and stages, with waves of progress, milestones, and challenges. I will advise you on recognizing the milestones (and insist you celebrate) and help you to overcome challenges, in upcoming chapters. To maximize progress and minimize challenges, read and follow the book chapters in order, understanding background information, concepts, and new terms. Then learn the prerequisite and teaching skills. Finally, learn the Human and Canine K9Signs in order, paying attention to the Tips and Comments sections.

Canine K9Sign is taught in two main phases: first the move, then the meaning. The move phase focuses on inspiring your dog to make the move. Next, you must get the move to occur on cue, where you can command the move. The second phase focuses on facilitating your dog to associate the move with its assigned new meaning. Two students are involved here, you and your dog. Fortunately you can learn the move, gesture, or sign from reading. The tools you use to teach yourself to sign might include imagination, imitation, reasoning, and direction. But you will have to teach your dog using other tools, such as trial-and-error, shaping, targeting, and modeling.

Teaching a move is much like teaching a trick. There are many ways to teach the moves. The technique depends on how easy or hard the dog finds the move. Small and energetic dogs might find moving a paw to the top of the head easy; large and older dogs may not. The easy ones are taught using luring with common stimuli, waiting for trial-and-error, mimicking, or cueing with known tricks. For example, to teach a move of "paw up," you can put your hand out with food. Some dogs will naturally paw the food. For another dog, this might not work. In this case, tapping her paw with your foot might provoke her to lift her paw. Difficult moves are taught using modeling, various objects to provoke the move, or shaping and other methods. Coming up with techniques to provoke the dog to make a move is challenging, fun, and rewarding for you and the dog. I enjoy this challenge immensely, and it helps me understand my dogs better.

More difficult moves are taught with shaping, imitating, targeting, and with a clicker. To promote a behavior (a move) to occur more often, you must provide a positive reinforcement after the behavior. This means after your dog performs a move, reward your dog. Your dog will then make the move more often to get that reward. Positive reinforcement is useful for teaching new moves and skills, improving a move or gesture, and maintaining that gesture. As your student learns gestures, she may generalize and use that gesture at other unexpected times. Observe carefully—she may be doing something useful for future signing.

Teaching the meaning of a move is significant and important, though for some dogs it can be a more challenging step. It requires a shift of perspective on the part of the dog. In the beginning when your dog makes an appropriate gesture, she teaches and tells you to produce what she perceives to be the meaning of a gesture—the reward. Once an animal has learned the meaning of the gesture, then it's up to her to gesture on her own (even when the object meaning isn't present). This converts the gesture into a sign—exactly what you want.

Dogs that have been taught to alert can be of even more assistance if they also know how to sign. While training a dog to alert, you teach a dog to alert *to* something, that is, to run between the object and you. The same behavior is essentially used for many alerts. But when teaching an assistance dog to sign, you'd teach the dog a different sign for each different alert. You wouldn't have to wonder what the problem is—your dog would tell you. For example, in K9Sign you would teach the dog to sign *Phone* when the phone rings, sign

Fire when fire is present, sign *Fire Truck* when that arrives, and *Water* when the faucet is dripping. Alerting is general; K9Signing is specific.

K9Signs are taught in a logical, rule-based format to increase the potential that the dog can figure out new signs herself and even alert you to things you never taught her. The language signs are a part of a structured, ordered system rather than a miscellaneous collection of random signs. Language lessons can extend the ability of animals to communicate what they already sense. In humans, language learning helps distinguish, clarify, and develop our thought process. Perhaps learning K9Sign Language can do the same for the canine thought process.

Milestones: Milestones are the visible "aha" improvements or jumps in your or your pet's learning, response to questions, gesture, or sign use. Some students tiptoe, others blast through different lessons and stages. The joy you experience and the praise you give will carry you and your dog through both the milestones and the challenges. Journal these experiences for future delight.

Jumps in learning and understanding will occur at various times. One of these leaps will certainly happen when your student realizes that not every move brings the same treat. Moving the left paw gets food, moving the right gets a toy. Another milestone will occur when your dog, looking at you for guided feedback, deliberately adjusts its paw-move as you say *Yeah* and, finally, moving correctly, hears you say *Yes!* She stops, you deliver a treat. What fun! Your dog will learn that through guided feedback, you will steer her to the correct move and will give her a terrific treat. What teamwork! Another milestone might come when your dog calmly signs *Potty* in front of you then escorts you to the door. As you open it, she runs out and poops in the proper place. These are signing moments to celebrate. This is the beginning of language.

Challenges: Challenges are the difficulties, mistakes, or stagnations you and your pets might encounter as you expand communication. Consider challenges as potential milestones, many being predictable. Your dogs will learn something in every lesson, but that something may not be what you planned. Be flexible. Make use of any learning that occurs. Assume a neutral attitude toward challenges and your pet will do the same. Animals will copy you. If you are calm about mistakes, so will your dog be. If you become frustrated (whether you show it or not), your dog will be too. Through each challenge, you will discover how she learns and responds. And you will discover that working through difficult lessons is a skill in itself. Don't give up; document, plan, back up to a successful lesson, reread, and reteach. For additional feedback and exchange, connect with the AnimalSign Center, sign up for our e-newsletter, join our blog, or a K9Signer group.

Many predictable challenges have easy solutions. You may find it difficult to say and sign the Canine K9Signs. The solution is to only say their signs. Your dog may not move correctly for a particular sign. The solution is to try a different move enticer, perhaps practice in a different setting, or choose a different mode (obedience, play). Your dog may not associate a move with its meaning. The solution may be to use a different object that represents the meaning or teach in a different setting. You may discover that a K9Sign move is identical to a command move you already use, confusing your dog. The solution is to modify the K9Sign just enough to avoid confusion. Experience with my clients has proven that many challenges are avoidable simply by reading the entire book in sequence and *then* implementing the lessons, in the order presented. Many challenges are dealt with in the Gestuary, especially the Tips or Comments sections.

Chal quit working for a while, in between learning *Food* and *Toy*. We had to back up and work in smaller steps; then one day she understood the difference between these signs. She kept signing *Food* when I showed her a toy. I didn't say a word, nor did I reward her. She lay down on the ground and looked up at me, seeming to say, *I Give Up.* So we calmly backtracked to practice signs she knew (and was treated for). Later we tried different approaches to learning *Toy.* Finally, after positioning myself just to her right, she used her right leg and finally understood that *Toy* was different from *Food.* Now she loves using *Toy* to entice me to throw a toy. One day when my cat AngelFur was sitting on the couch, I asked Chal *What's That?* Chal signed *Toy.* Thank goodness not *Food.* This sign selection was significant, giving me insight into her thinking. She communicated that she thought of my cat (at least in that moment), as a toy, not food. Later, Chal learned signs for living creatures such as *Cat.* Now when I ask her *What's That?* she signs *Cat* with her appropriate left hind leg, the body part used for living creatures.

Teach or reteach a skill that helps your student overcome challenges, and do this immediately after the challenging moment. When dealing with unpleasant emotions or behaviors, such as frustration or lying down when you attempt to move a body part, be very careful what you do before and after these expressions. Students will associate their emotions and behaviors with what happens before and after an event. For example, with frustration, be aware of what prompts it and what you do after it is displayed. You can prevent frustration, by steering the lesson *before* the frustration occurs. For example, if you are teaching the move for *Toy* (right front leg up and down) and your dog keeps using her left leg, you don't say *No* but just don't treat for this. You try other ways to get her to move her right leg, finally your dog starts looking away, breathing harder, or may just make a small sign she is going to lie down—quickly do something she enjoys: pleasantly distract her, manually move her right leg, then say *Yes! Toy* and reward her, ask her to do something she knows (and can be treated for) such as sign *Food.* You don't want frustration to creep in, thwart it before it happens. You will learn to spot the subtle indicators of frustration. Signing must be fun. After seeing frustration in your dog, back up and reteach in smaller, success-promoting steps. But do not make a fuss of frustration, and definitely do not reward it. If I had given Chal a treat after she displayed frustration, she would have learned to associate frustration with getting a treat. She'd be inclined to show frustration often. When Chal becomes frustrated, I back up and teach a smaller part of the attempted lesson, to promote success. This way Chal learns how to turn frustration into success, that is, do some small part of the lesson. This also works with humans overwhelmed by a huge project. Break a large project down into small tasks, succeed at each, and reward until the project is completed.

A particularly interesting challenge appears as a dog tries to understand what you are doing with all your movements. Your hand, head, and body movements flare while you are signing. Are you asking her to: *Do Something* or *Imitate* or *Try* or *Name* or *Create* (a new gesture) or *Sign* or what? Are you signing to her or to someone else? K9Sign has gestures that give context to your moves, letting the animal know what you are doing. Some dogs may figure out your intentions quickly, others need to be cued in. Sample cue-ins that you will learn are *Sign* (command), *Try* (command), *Attend* (look/listen), *IS* (implies the statement *That IS Name), Not You* (gestures are not for you), and *What?* and *Who?* Picking out the signs from the simple movements is engaging work, but worth every word.

Teaching

As a language educator, you'll be planning, preparing, and holding class with lessons. You'll need to gain the skill, qualities, and techniques of good teachers and trainers. Strive to develop these qualities and use these techniques with your dogs. Good teachers know the subject they will teach. This means you need to read this book and perhaps other recommended books as you proceed. Good teachers have mastered behavior management (obedience) and provide constant monitoring (observation and analysis) and give feedback. They make clear the expectations by having a goal in mind, and they establish rules. They provide consistent consequences, not only rewards for behavior. They exude a high-expectation attitude, and provide a positive and supportive learning environment. No punishment is given, so students feel safe to learn, to explore, and to make mistakes while trying, discovering, and being creative. Teachers can explicitly teach or guide discovery. Good teachers have lesson plans (lesson subject, goals, and methods) and teach with a facilitating and fun (paws-on) approach. They constantly observe and check for understanding (CFU), assessing what the student knows and doesn't know. The teachers adapt lessons accordingly (backing or speeding up, changing direction, or quitting for the day). They use appropriate methods to address student needs—especially addressing what students don't know. Teachers may need to reteach in smaller steps, with more patience. Good teachers take breaks and reward, for their and their student's well-being.

Good trainers have many of the above qualities, though some are phrased differently for training purposes. Training animals requires some different approaches, depending on the training type. In class, good trainers watch the environment, people, and dogs. The instructors clearly convey expectations, set reachable goals, and adjust their methods to maximize success. They give feedback and reward (both human and animal) the desired response. They manage and respond to unwanted behavior, quickly and appropriately. Trainers are quick to adapt, or even stop, the lesson to respond to their students as needed. A critical skill for trainers is to know when to check for understanding (CFU) in the human and animal students. If either doesn't understand an explanation or instruction, the appropriate learning won't happen and frustration will ensue. Everyone must be attentive, learning, and on task. When the trainer can assure all this happens in a fun environment, that's when the best learning occurs. Who wouldn't want to go back to that class?

With your good teacher and trainer skills, plan your many lessons, though some spontaneous lessons will always occur. Planning involves thinking through the lesson, the environment, clarifying the goal, expectations, breaking it down into steps, and strategizing how to deal with your animal's needs and challenges. Before beginning the lesson, it is essential that you read through the entire signing lesson, including the Tips and Comments. (I do not recommend reading the lesson for the first time while your dog is in class.)

Prepare for your planned lesson by having accessible all your needed items—objects, tools, clickers, people, and treats—in the class environment. Practice the lesson in your mind or with a willing friend, if needed. Then invite your dog to the lesson with the sign *Class.*

In class, give simple lessons using key ideas in learning, teaching, and practicing gestures. Follow the explicit instructions in the K9Sign Gestuary, but be flexible and adapt lessons using a variety of strategies, depending on what is, or is not, evolving. Be sure to always end the lesson with a fun, positive-learning experience, and sign *Class Finished.* After the lesson, use the learned signs in meaningful ways throughout the day. Reinforce the sign session in informal lessons.

Master K9Sign Language by embracing the qualities and skills of a professional teacher or trainer and you will enhance the ability for you and your dog to communicate. Tutor your dog as a part of daily life, and communication will blossom into language.

Observing

As we discussed in chapter 3, observation is a key skill. The field of ethology directs us to concentrate on observable, documentable behaviors, distinct from interpretations of behaviors, which attribute to animals' feelings, thoughts, and intentions. You can see a dog lift its paw one foot off the ground. This could be a simple reach, or it could mean *Food.* We could presume, but in reality we don't know the dog's intention. With K9Sign, we will knowingly take that presumptuous leap in order to promote language development. We respond to gestures, as though, in case they are signs.

During a lesson, people tend to be preoccupied with their own goals and actions rather than with observing their dog. Teacher development programs often have an observer watching the class, then noting their observations. Having an additional person observe you and your dog to describe or document the scene can help illuminate the actual events. Teachers videotape class lessons for peer review, promoting teacher growth. Videotaping interactions with your dog and then reviewing the tape as an observer reveals behaviors you might have otherwise ignored. While with your animal student, consciously observe her behavior and body part movements, looking for communication. Most likely you'll see more than you can decipher. (Record that!) Periodically (daily, weekly, during difficult sessions, etc.), audio- or videotape the lessons for archiving and reviewing your journey. These will provide memorable and valuable feedback about you and your dog's behaviors.

Kelly, a student, and I were talking when Chal came into the room and tapped a storage drawer with her nose. I presumed there was food in the drawer. Kelly noticed Chal lifting her right front leg, which is the sign for an object. I asked **What?** Chal lifted her right paw, flicking it slightly, the sign for keys. I was puzzled, I had expected her to sign for food. I opened the drawer and saw no food, but there it was, the key to her yard gate. As I reached into the drawer, Chal ran out to her gate, waiting for me to open it. Without Kelly present to observe and call my attention to Chal's behavior, I was expecting something else, and might have missed this communication. This also points out how expectations influence what we pay attention to. I was expecting the other leg to move and was not as attentive to her entire body—her vocabulary tool.

Journaling

Journaling will be a useful tool to highlight milestones and aid in overcoming challenges. When you feel blocked from progress, reread your journal and reflect. Insights and ideas will abound. Journaling is also useful for exchanging information with others. If you pursue consulting with the AnimalSign Center about your signing dog, I'll be asking you to share your observations, which will be more accurately found in your journal entries than in your memory.

CHAPTER 5

Before You Teach K9Sign

Dog enthusiasts from varying backgrounds have expressed interest in teaching their dogs to communicate with K9Sign. These people are pet lovers, companions, caregivers, trainers, sitters, volunteers, and veterinary professionals. They bring their unique backgrounds, skills, and perspectives to the teaching of language to animals. Many have already taught their pets (and their pets have taught them) tricks and simple communications. Whatever your background, this chapter will guide you as your canine's language teacher. As a teacher, you'll learn about having high expectations, lesson planning and holding class, as well as the need for practice, and quizzing and testing your students. You'll learn the value of journaling, where you document the K9Sign language development and experiences of your canine student.

Some animal trainers consider themselves as teachers and actually teach while they train. But there are important differences between those who primarily train and those who primarily teach. Many trainers work with, and focus on, the physical procedures and skills; teachers work to develop a variety of skills and knowledge. They expect that animals will perform on command; teachers expect that too, but strive to develop the animal's ability to think and communicate creatively and independently. For true language, creative and independent signing is essential. I approach animals as an animal language educator, focusing on developing their cognitive and, specifically, their language skills. While teaching K9Sign, approach your animals as a teacher, an educator, rather than a trainer looking only for obedience.

High Expectations

Teachers' expectations are a critical factor for human student learning. This is likely true for canine students as well. Have high goals and expectations as you teach your dog to sign, but be supportive of your student's actual learning capabilities, experimentation, and performance. A way to achieve this creative and useful mindset is to consider the following questions: How would you approach teaching your human child a gestural language? What if she had a different body structure (say like a canine)? What if she had genius-level, unique perceptions or motor skills such as running or jumping? What if she had heightened perception of some senses (olfaction—smell), but was challenged in others? What if she could hear a higher pitch or at a lower volume than most children, or perhaps was deaf or hard-of-hearing? What if the shape of her mouth prevented her from talking the way you do, but she could produce other sounds? What if she understood and anticipated much of what you did but didn't respond to elaborate phrases? Regardless, you'd probably want your child to develop and gain language skills at whatever level she had the potential for. Perhaps you'd enroll her in a special school or course to help her develop her potential and overcome challenges. If you envision your dog student in this same way, teaching her K9Sign will be an incredible adventure. You will discover a world of communication previously unavailable and hidden from you.

For those of you who prefer a more realistic approach, another mental framework can be just as productive. Most of you know how to communicate with babies and children through the exchange of natural signs. With a baby, you will expect, look for, and respond to body moves as communications. If a baby reaches out and points in the direction of a toy, you expect she wants it, and respond by saying "toy" and giving it to her. If he starts tearing a placemat and you shake your finger left to right, the child might stop tearing it. Some of you may also have language proficiency with American Sign Language, communicating with formal signs. Approach your canine student with this mental framework of expecting communication and interpreting gestures. This will raise your expectations and patience as you open the world of words to your pet. Both mind-sets are anthropomorphic but harmless, and they potentially increase the opportunity for your dogs to learn. As these mind-sets influence your attitude, they also affect your student's learning.

Dr. Duane Rumbaugh of the Great Ape Trust Research Center found that, with chimpanzees, a teacher's expectations of their learning performance plays an important role in how much they learn. If we don't teach with high expectations, we cloak our student's potential. Though my personal expectations are high, my science and quality assurance backgrounds caution me about making *interpretations* of my students' performance. What students perform, or do, is objective, but their performance can be cued by something I'm doing, whether I know it or not. What I *think* dogs are thinking is actually my interpretation of their performance. The performance is fact, but a particular interpretation may, or may not, be valid. Over the next few years, I expect scientific studies will track canine performance and guide us to insightful interpretations. Meanwhile I teach, gather data, and proceed on—communicating with my signing students.

As you teach K9Sign to your dogs, convey (at least initially) that they can do no wrong; any sign is a good sign. Yes, this feedback will be an exaggeration of the truth, but your dogs must not fear trying or making mistakes. When they do err, either don't say anything or give guiding feedback. As your dogs learn, they will gain confidence. Let them figure some things out and gain the assurance that they may experiment with moves without negative outcomes. Creativity requires this freedom. Reward them for trying. This concept of trying is so important, that it has its own gesture—*Try.*

....

Imagine! Trip, a Seeing Eye dog, is walking his human companion, Brad. Approaching a step down in the path, Trip stops, then taps Brad's knee (K9Sign for **Step-Down**), a few minutes later they reach a slant down in the road, again Trip stops, but this time taps Brad's ankle (K9Sign for **Slant**). This enables Brad to walks smoothly along the road. Trip sees Brad's friend Molly approaching, so Trip stops to brush Brad's right knee (K9Sign for **Molly**). Brad says, "Hi Molly."

....

During language lessons, find ways to communicate *Yes!* Do not use the word *No.* It has a negative flavor which you don't want contaminating creative language learning. Instead, to indicate that a move is wrong, keep silent or say/sign *Na* sweetly. This is a nice way of saying *Not What I Want, Keep Trying.* Guide your students to the correct move. Don't let them stress about making incorrect gestures. Your language students will thrive with your high expectations, coupled with a positive, creative attitude. Your dogs will use the signs you've taught them and jump ahead to create new signs, which they will be teaching *you.*

Class

To communicate with K9Sign, you and your dogs need to learn the signs in (and out of) class. Plan and prepare the class space or area. On some days class may be inside, other days outside. At first, select a quiet place with no distractions. Have a desk, room, table, chair or area and supplies ready. The supplies you'll need are this book, your journal, a variety of treats, bowls, a leash, toys, and objects. At times you'll also want to have assistants, a clicker, and perhaps even a mirror (for you and your student to watch yourselves), video cam, or tape recorder. As you prepare for class, have your goal in mind—to communicate using the learned gestures as signs. The goal should always be that your dog will make the correct gesture, and then associate the gesture with the meaning.

Chal has many class areas. One area has a small desk with cards, toys, and countable objects, and a cabinet holding a variety of treats and clickers. Sometimes class occurs spontaneously in different areas: by a room door, her crate, near the fireplace, in front of my car, or outside. To teach her the names of different rooms in the house, of course we need to go to the room. Sometimes Chal starts class, sometimes I do. Initially Chal wanted less time with the lessons, but over the years she wants more and more. She communicates *Class* by sitting at her desk waiting for me, sometimes politely tapping me to remind me to hold a class lesson.

Lessons

To conduct lessons, you will need to master several preparatory skills. You'll need the prerequisite dog obedience skills, a solid understanding of the appropriate teaching methods, and proficiency with both the Human and Canine K9Signs. In chapter 9, you'll find the Model Teaching Instructions on page 119 from which you'll teach your student her signs, one at a time, in the order presented. Teach the Basic/Foundation signs first, then the Intermediate signs. Try the Advanced signs last. Practice the signs yourself, then plan and implement how you will teach them to your dog. You'll both need to practice until signing becomes second nature, and your second language.

Prerequisite obedience skills are necessary. Make sure you and your dog have basic obedience down, and that your dog is comfortable with you handling her body. If you need help mastering these skills, use the resources found in the reference section of this book or in bookstores, or take a local obedience training class. Understand your role as a teacher, and the skills you should gain.

To hold canine language lessons, master the Human K9Signs that you communicate to your student. Your student will develop a receptive understanding of those words. These signs enable you instruct and guide as you teach your dog how to sign herself. I use the Human K9Signs throughout the K9Sign Model Teaching Instructions and Gestuary.

The Canine K9Sign lessons, using the procedures in the Model Teaching Instructions, provide the specific sign lesson (teaching the move and the meaning), as well as Practice Exercises, Tips, and Comments. Perform these lessons in the order instructed. Start with beginning signs first, then teach the intermediate signs. Don't skip around, as you may either end up unsuccessful or with only a few learned tricks, or worse, with you both frustrated. Within each lesson, I guide you through the concepts and gestures—the critical building blocks for communication and language development. You are making an important investment in your dog's cognitive development and ability to communicate. Take your time and enjoy.

In an AnimalSign class, a human student said she had trouble with teaching **Food** and **Toy**. Both she and her dog were confused and frustrated. She couldn't attend all the classes and could only browse the course book, *AnimalSign to You!* With little time, she eagerly jumped right to the signs she wanted to teach, skipping all the preliminary steps. She tried to teach the signs **Food** and **Toy** in one session. Consequently she became frustrated, and her dog didn't learn either sign. This type of problem is easily avoided. It's important to wait until you have time; then go for it from the beginning to succeed.

The concentrated time for teaching a lesson should be short, ten to fifteen minutes. Repeat these short sessions several times a day. While you teach in small steps, constantly check for understanding (CFU is the popular teaching acronym for this). Is your student looking at you, attending to you, seeing and hearing what you are doing? Does she seem to understand what you are doing, saying, and expecting? Are you pausing, respecting her cognitive processing time? If your answer is no, then your student probably isn't learning nor enjoying the lesson.

Each prepared lesson should be small, short, clear, and simple. Each should be presented in an upbeat manner, beginning and ending clearly. Capture your dog's attention, then indicate that the lesson is starting. Demonstrate what you will teach, then teach it using CFU, and modify the lesson as needed. Give ample feedback and find ways to reward. Help your prize student succeed, and always end with a successful task (even a sit). If your last trial didn't work, go back to one that did, praise, reward, then end. After class, do something fun but calm. Calm, so your dog's brain can process the previous lesson without distraction. This also allows short-term memory (the lesson that just happened) to begin its eventual consolidation into long-term memory (fixing of memory). Fun, so your dog associates class with something pleasant. She will enjoy and learn more in class.

The beginning lessons are intended to be interesting to your pets. Dogs become increasingly interested in signing as they experience that signing enables them to have more control of their environment. One older dog, Rosie, was not interested in the lessons, and was even fearful or suspicious of signing. Though she responded positively to me and to treats, as soon as I'd start a lesson she'd give me a strange look and leave to go to "sleep" on the couch. My older horse, Chazz, was not interested in learning signs either; he wanted the treats for free. But he watched me teach Princess, my signing horse, with focused interest. My cats preferred to observe signing, but allowed me to communicate with them using basic signs and other creative methods. Teach signing to animals who are willing to learn. Do not force it on those not interested. Do give them time to explore signing under positive conditions. The uninterested ones may just change their mind. When you see interest, sign at the chance.

Practice

Once a lesson has been learned, practice the sign with your dog, but be sure you are practicing correctly. Practice after class in a variety of places and conditions, during play or at rest. Practice formally and informally, while performing daily activities such as watching TV, working at your computer, reading, or relaxing. Signing to your dogs often may inspire them to sign to you. Watch for new learning and new signs, which can appear during practice. Be sensitive to how much your dog can effectively practice. A rule to follow is, if you dog enjoys it and wants to continue, do so (if you have the endurance). Otherwise, keep the practice to a few successful minutes. Dogs need and can tolerate different amounts of practice. Keep your dogs happy.

Laila, a brilliant boxer puppy, and her person, Laurie, had just learned to sign **Food** in an AnimalSigning class. At home one night, a family member was on the couch eating. Laila went over, sat, then signed **Food.** Though Laila didn't get a response for her communication, it would have been a great teaching moment. Fortunately Laila wasn't discouraged. She then signed **Food** to Laurie, who responded.

Quizzing

After mastering a sign, gently quiz the learning. I use the word *quizzing* differently than *testing*. Quizzing is proofing. Here you would ask your dog to sign words in different places, with and without distraction, with you in different positions and locations, and to sign with other people. You will reinforce the sign and help the dog generalize it. It is beyond the initial teaching, but not quite testing. Testing (dealt with later) needs more than one sign so you can help and test the dog's differentiation of signs. Quiz only after your students really perform the sign correctly for days. Quiz by asking for, and reinforcing, the sign in different situations (in various rooms, with various distractions, with you in different positions). Quizzing helps your dog focus, generalize, and clarify the sign's meaning. During quizzing, you can communicate that you don't want your dog to sign during an event or competition. A dog signing for food in the middle of an obedience class might cause her to flunk the test. A dog being handled by a judge should not sign until after the judge leaves. Practice and quiz your dog on not signing during these events. Do so by sweetly, saying **Not Now** or **Finished**. Don't use **No,** so as not to discourage signing in general.

After teaching and quizzing one sign well, start teaching another sign. Don't confuse your student by teaching two signs at once. Your student is learning a gesture with underlying concepts, and this takes processing time. In fact, there may be a long delay (even weeks) before your dog shows evidence of learning. Bauman discusses a similar prelearning stage in dogs during training sessions. All your teaching may appear futile, but suddenly one day learning will be evident. This delay is observed in babies learning baby signs. It's normal. I've seen in this in many signing students. Stay focused, keep learning while having fun. Stay motivated by documenting any behavior changes, as you wait for the sign to appear.

Quizzing should be a positive learning experience. If your dog isn't performing signs, then go back and reteach. Make sure your dog passes quizzes before testing, which is more demanding and rigorous. Set your dog up for success.

Testing

Testing your dog means asking her to provide correct gestures for many objects. Testing also provides a means of further learning and clarifying meaning. Individually test each sign, for the move and the meaning, in a variety of situations. After your dog has mastered several individual gestures well, have her regularly compare and contrast pairs of gestures.

After you teach individual signs, compare them for your student. Compare very different objects and moves (right side versus left side, back leg versus front leg). For example, after learning **Food** and **Toy,** test your student by having food and toy present. Point to the food and ask **What's That?** She should sign **Food** with her left front leg. Then point to the toy and ask **What's That?** She should sign **Toy** with her right front leg. Guide her if she doesn't, by reiterating the correct sign. If you show food and she signs *Toy*, say/sign *Na, IS Food. Sign Food.* When she does, reward her.

After testing signs using different legs, contrast signs made with the same body part. Compare *Ball* and *Frisbee.* Both signs use the right front leg. Point to the ball and ask your dog *What Type IS That?* She should sign *Ball* with her right front leg bent. Then point to the Frisbee and ask *What Type IS That?* She should sign *Frisbee* with her right front leg up high. Guide her if she doesn't by modeling the correct sign. If you show the ball and she signs *Frisbee,* say/sign *Na, IS Ball. Sign Ball.* When she does, reward her.

After you teach several names, contrast the names of several people, using *Who's That?* If she is not successful, work with her to clarify. Back up to previous lessons if your dog is confused. Reteach if she still doesn't get it. Proceed after your dog is successful. Testing and reteaching contrasting signs helps to clarify the differences and similarities between signs. With this clarity, she might understand the purpose and power of signing.

Chal took a while to demonstrate the distinction between the specific term *Rope* and the general term *Toy.* Several sessions with me and the rope in various locations, while contrasting the two signs with questions *What?* and *What Type?* paid off. During excited play, before I threw a rope, I signed/said *What?* She clearly gestured *Toy.* Then I asked her *What Type?* She clearly gestured *Rope.* We played with the rope until she wanted to quit—a long-time reward.

Journaling

Keeping a journal is an important, dynamic learning tool. It helps you to observe, track responses, evaluate, resolve issues, and plan. Viewing events as a teacher, journal the lessons. Note the goal of the lesson and the accomplishments, challenges, unusual events (and your interpretation of them), and other observations you feel are important. Note the quiz, test events, and their results. Include additional comments, posing imaginative questions: What would an observing teacher say? What do you think your dog would say about your teaching? What could she be thinking about her performance, and feeling about her challenges? Reflection on your journal can help you strategize and guide your next lesson.

I use journaling to know what to do next, what to fix about my teaching. In particular, I like to imagine what Chal would have to say about my lessons. She might say *Too Fast* or *Too Slow* or *What Are You Doing? One Thing At A Time Please* or *More, Change Treats, You're Doing It Wrong.* Perhaps during other lessons, she'd say *Nice, I Like This, Do It My Way, Keep Going, What's Next? How About This Move, Let Me Try Something.* With these questions, I'm playing with my own intuition and perceptions, not Chal's, but I find this process helps expose my teaching mistakes and strengths. Clearly I am unconsciously aware of doing things a certain way, perhaps even rushing the learning process. Writing things down highlights my actions and intentions, and makes them easier for me to objectively address and change. Using imagination can improve your skills and lessons.

Tracking: Document your journal in multiple formats: written text, spreadsheet, tables, and video and tape recordings. Supplement written documents with video or tape. Label everything in detail. This makes reviewing easy.

Observing: Writing down your observations enables you to observe your pet's communications. Document both irregular and regular observations. You may not know their significance till later. You may discover something important. Say you are teaching one sign, but your dog signs something new. You may think she didn't succeed, but she might have been communicating. By documenting your observations, you'll be able to identify these important moments (especially if they happen often). Noting observations helps you follow the evolution of communications. If you don't journal, you'll not only forget the exact details and miss important milestones, you'll miss communication patterns that are evolving. Seeing observations in written form can be useful and enlightening.

Evaluating: Rereading the journal will enable you to evaluate the lessons, your actions, and your dog's responses. This helps you to solve problems and to recognize achievements and areas needing improvement. You'll better understand you and your dog's learning style. Perhaps you'll notice that your dog doesn't pay attention well in the morning, but is great at night. You might be surprised to discover that your dog makes a new gesture after certain events, or your dog learns better when you are quiet rather than loud. If you seek professional assistance, offering the journal entries will help your professional consultant understand your situation.

Planning: After evaluating a past lesson, you can better plan the next. Plan how to entice your dog to use the new sign she made up. Plan how to best address any problems that might recur with various approaches. Backtrack to what worked, and break down the sessions into smaller chunks. Practice by yourself before reteaching your dog. Note changes in your dog's response to your new teaching approach.

Example: I recommend that you journal using a spreadsheet or Word document with a table of several columns. This way you can sort by column, and you can see trends easily.

1. Date of Record
2. Method (teaching method you planned or actually used)
3. Goal (desired learning)
4. Event (expected and unexpected events before, after, during the session)
5. Challenges (problems)
6. Fix (ways to get around challenges)
7. Comments (anything else noteworthy about yourself, your dog, and the session)

Event documentations are particularly important. An event can be something that was successful or not, puzzling, fascinating, or troubling. Keep in mind that observations are distinct from your interpretation and should be documented separately. The former is what you sense and perceive, the latter is what you think or assume your observation means. One can be true and the other false (and vice versa). In case you are wrong about your interpretations, your observations will still be there in original form to guide you in another direction.

In the Events column, write down the following:

1. Describe what you observed/sensed, not what you think it means. Do not interpret. (Example: Her head and leg moved up.)
2. The context in which this occurred. (Example: In the quiet kitchen, I signed/said ***What's That?*** and lifted food above her head.)

3. Describe one observation with the interpretation where you assume communication occurred. (Example: She understood and signed *Food.*)

4. Describe one observation with the interpretation where you assume a communication did *not* occur. Your dog wasn't communicating but just moving. (Example: She may not know the meaning of food yet. But she lifted her foot because her leg was reaching for the food. She wasn't signing *Food.*)

In the Challenge column, note the difficulties, problems, and mistakes you or your dogs encounter or make. Challenges offer an opportunity for improvement. Detail what you observe and interpret the challenge to mean.

The Fix column is for you to note what you think you will try to do to fix the problem. List ideas you get from other people or books.

The Comments column is for other thoughts, ideas, and reflections. Include how other people and animals respond to your dog when she signs. Add what you think and how you feel about the process. Note the evolution of your thinking about communicating with your dog and other dogs.

• •

Imagine! A search and rescue (SAR) dog named Sun has K9Sign Language training. On a search and rescue, Sun searches and finds several people stuck in a cave under rubble. Sun returns to her handler, Mark. She barks and K9Signs, **People 4, Direction There** (pointing left). Mark signs **How Many?** Sun signs **4.** Mark asks, **What Type?** Sun responds, **Male 1, Female 2, Child 1.** Mark asks, **How Far?** Sun signs **Leaps 10.** Mark signs **Blood?** Sun replies **Yes, Blood, Blood.** Mark signs **Got It**. Mark informs the team they need more resources, and they later rescue the trapped victims.

CHAPTER 6

• •

Before Your Dog Learns K9Sign

Before attempting to teach K9Sign to your dog, be sure you and your dog have mastered the prerequisite obedience commands and that you have skill in recognizing achievements and providing timely feedback and reinforcements. Using the clicker to mark a successful event, and to indicate a reward is coming, is useful and highly recommended but not essential. This chapter and chapters 7 and 8, are critical components to building an expanding vocabulary, the framework for potential language development. Resist the temptation to skip these chapters and jump to the K9Sign Gestuary.

Obedience

To learn K9Sign, you and your dogs must have mastered some obedience commands. If you haven't, find a book, class, or trainer near you before you proceed. The obedience commands dogs need include *Sit, Stand, Down, Stay, Come, Leave It,* and most importantly, *Attend.* High-energy dogs need a lot of work on these important skills. Attention is critical, as you'll be showing your dog what to do, what to look at, how to move. Your dog needs to be watching you, undistracted. Both humans and dogs learn what they attend to. Your dog must also be comfortable with you handling her body, especially her limbs and head. If your dog knows how to target an object, that will be a great help.

Feedback

As your dog learns new skills, she will require feedback that will let her know how she is doing so she can adjust, as needed. She'll know how close or how far she is from doing what you want. You need to know how to communicate the feedback: what form and when to give it, how often and for how long. Many of you already know how to give basic feedback with **Good** or **Yes!** Most nontrainers know how to communicate these basic words, but may say the words too late, leaving the dog with a misconception of the exact behavior that was desired. This book will help you build on your basic skills so that you become proficient at the specific feedback words to use, when, and how to use them.

The feedback **Yes!** alone doesn't motivate an animal to strive to perform behaviors you want. Through repeatedly pairing **Yes!** with an appearing treat, **Yes!** becomes much like a treat. **Yes!** becomes associated with a reinforcement, a reward such as a treat. Now the conditioned **Yes!** helps motivate an animal to do what you ask. The animal learns to behave as you want in order to gain more control of its environment, in this case get something it wants—a reward. With repetition, your dog learns the behavior you rewarded as a habit.

A terrific technique using a clicker method was introduced to the dog world by Karen Pryor in her book *Don't Shoot the Dog!* Use this method when teaching new gestures (especially the move). Through apparent brain activation, the click increases motivation and speeds up learning. The click sound marks the moment the dog makes the correct move and communicates that to the dog. In addition (after you train this association), the click signifies that positive reinforcement, a reward, is coming. Use this technique just as your dog performs a wanted behavior (gesture), then give the reinforcement—the reward. This technique is symbolized in this book with Click ‡ Reward (click then reward). Try it on yourself with a friend. Have the friend click when you do something she wants, then she should reward you with a small treat (jelly bean, perhaps?). After you perform what she wants, hearing a click alerts you to exactly what you did, helps you remember that action, and the treat motivates you to do it again.

Say/sign **Yes!** just before the click to enhance the power of **Yes!** For example: **Yes!** ‡ Click ‡ Treat. The **Yes!** implies the click, which implies the reward. Learning this sequence, the dog will anticipate the next item in the chain. Eventually the **Yes!** alone implies reward. After a gesture is learned, you can fade out the click and just use **Yes!** ‡ Reward. Give rewards regularly for correct behavior; later give rewards only occasionally. Remember, if you click, you must reward, but you may say **Yes!** or just reward without the click. After your dog masters a new move, trick, gesture, or sign, the clicker is no longer needed for that sign. Using **Yes!** on occasion is sufficient. Use the clicker for other new signs. Once you are comfortable using the clicker, teaching new gestures with this tool is easier.

Reinforcements/Rewards

Teach gestures with a positive approach using rewards. Have plenty of a—not too expensive—generic food. This is a food you will not specifically name (other than as a general **Food**). Use this food to teach the general **Food** sign and the nonfood gestures, such as **Toy.** Some special foods you'll specifically name, such as the sign **Chicken.** Over time, your dog will understand that the generic food reward is just a reward, *not* the object or food you are naming. When you are teaching gestures for special foods (chicken or liver), use that specific food as the reward. As you teach **Chicken,** reward with the chicken.

This same reward concept applies to teaching the general concept for a small object, such as **Toy,** versus specific small object **Ball.** When you are teaching the sign **Ball,** a specific toy, use that ball as the reward (if your dog really likes balls). If your dog does not particularly like balls, then reward with the ball, followed immediately by the generic food reward.

Initially your dog will need reinforcements (rewards) to be motivated to display learned behaviors—to sign. Eventually I hope your dog will see the value of communicating with K9Signs as its own reward and simply sign as an extension of her natural gesturing.

CHAPTER 7

How to Teach Human K9Signs to Your Dog

The Human K9Sign Gestuary explains the gestures that you will sign to your dog. Your dog will use receptive language skills to understand what you are communicating. She will learn the sign meanings from practice and consistent use, in specific contexts. These Human K9Signs are necessary to teach your dog to sign to you.

The Human K9Signs, which you will sign and say (sign/say), are categorized as indicators, statements, feedback, requests, and questions. The words have specific meanings and also provide the situation's context. The Human K9Signs are:

- *Attend*
- *That*
- *Try*
- *What Type?*

- *Yah*
- *IS*
- *Freeze*
- *Who?*

- *Yes!*
- *Class*
- *Sign*

- *Na*
- *Finished*
- *What?*

Indicators: Imagine you are a dog, looking up at your human mother. Your mother is moving her hands, head, body, eyes, occasionally glancing at you (a dog), and talking in various tones into a phone. You might wonder in dog think: ***To Whom IS She Talking? Me? Phone? What IS She Saying/Signing? Should I Pay Attention, Listen, Learn A Name, Do Something?***

To deal with potential confusion, K9Sign uses indicators that are either signs by themselves or that accompany signs. Use indicators to clue dogs into the context so that they understand what is going on, what is expected of them, who is talking to whom, and what gesture type you are using. Your signing comments will vary. Sometimes you'll announce ***Class,*** or name an object (***IS Toy***), or make a request (***Sign***). The sign for ***Class*** will orient your dog to a learning session, thus preparing her cognitive functions for language learning. The sign ***IS*** orients your dog to an object you are naming, priming her for the next word—that she will be learning to sign. Then, when you request to her to ***Sign,*** she'll communicate to you. Repeated use of ***IS*** and ***Sign*** promotes receptive and productive signing.

Chal knows when I sign ***IS Word,*** for example ***IS Car*** and then manually move her body, she is supposed to repeat that move herself. When I say ***IS Car,*** she relinquishes her body to my molding. Sometimes I needn't even say ***Sign Car,*** she'll spontaneously repeat the move I molded. She's learned that ***IS Car,*** or any general ***IS*** word, means a learning session is going on. She's learned to learn.

Indicators help your dog figure out the scenarios. Be aware that sometimes you will move your hands without intending to sign. Your dog may respond, thinking you are signing. With indicators, your dog can better interpret your movements as signs or not.

Some animals will figure out your intentions on their own. Others will need to be cued in initially. For example, to indicate you are communicating with your dog and not with the other people in the room, look at and point to your dog, then sign ***That.*** (***That*** is an indicator sign that means you are calling attention to something, in this case, your dog). To indicate a question where you expect a response, tilt your head as you ask ***Who?, What?,*** or ***What Type?*** Use your voice to give other clues about a conversation. If you are naming something, sign/say ***IS*** with a confident tone; to request an action such as *Sit,* use a firm commanding tone. I include many tips and comments like this within the sign lessons.

Statements: Statements, though listed as single or multiple words, often imply sentences. These can be about events, objects, concepts, and even time. Examples are *That, IS Word,* and *Finished.*

Feedback: Feedback signs tell your student how close she is to reaching your request (*Na*, *Yah, Yeah*), or that she has reached it (*Yes!*). You'll need these signs to teach everything.

Requests: Requests (polite commands) tell your dog to do something, such as *Attend* or *Fetch.* Most often these are used for obedience, such as *Sit, Off, Stay.* These signs orient your dog to the activity type your dog should engage in. A particularly important request is to communicate—*Sign.*

Questions: Questions ask something and expect a response (*What?, Who?*). After your dog's signing skills are well developed, asking these questions can aid your teaching new signs quickly.

You, not your dog, will perform these Human K9Signs. But your dog will have to understand them. After you have mastered saying/signing Human K9Signs and your dog responds appropriately, use the signs to teach your dog her very own Canine K9Signs.

Human K9Sign Gestuary

The Human K9Sign Gestuary includes signs categorized as Statements, Feedback, Requests, and Questions. Each sign is presented in a consistent way: the Meaning in context, the Gesture and how to make it, the Correct Canine Response, a Sample Lesson, Practice Exercises, with Tips and Comments. The Move is what the gestures look like; how to make the move details what your body should do. The Meaning in context describes what the gestures symbolize (an object, an action, an adjective). The Correct Canine Response describes what your dog should do after you sign. The key section of each sign is the Sample Lesson, which demonstrates in steps how to use the sign and convey its meaning. The Practice Exercises provide various ways to learn and master the sign. The Tips section offers suggestions, things to watch out for, with special notes for different canine breeds, sizes, age, learning styles, temperaments, history, or other variables. The Comments provide other important notes.

As you teach, speak to your pet as you would to a baby, pronouncing each word part (consonants and vowels) clearly and loudly. Research led by Denis Burnham found that people tend to speak to dogs differently than to babies. People don't pronounce the vowels when speaking to dogs as well as they do when speaking to babies. This undoubtedly impacts dogs' opportunity to learn language. So it is not surprising that experts have also noted that dogs currently understand more consonants than vowels. Do dogs not understand vowels because of the lack of exposure to vowels, or because of lack of ability to recognize vowels? We don't know. So give your dog the benefit of the doubt and speak to your dog as you would to a baby or child, stressing vowels too: for **Ball,** say **Baaall.** Doing so potentially maximizes your dog's receptive word understanding as we know it does for our human babies.

The Human K9Sign Gestuary begins with the important request ***Attend***. Animals (humans included) must attend to learn anything, including language. The Gestuary continues with statements, feedback, other requests, and questions. Learn these in order, though some require you teach your dog a sign from the Canine K9Sign Gestuary. Then come back to this Human K9Sign Gestuary.

HUMAN SIGNING NOTATIONS

- "Object" or "object/event" stands for a variety of "things" including objects, events, situations, behaviors, etc.
- ***Word*** represents something to name. ***Word*** itself is not a sign. But the replacement for ***Word*** is. Replace ***Word*** with a specific, relevant object or event, such as ***Toy*** or ***Food.***
- I use sign/say ***Word*** often, as I instruct you. Your adherence to sign and say depends on whether you are using the Human K9Signs or working with the Canine K9Signs.
- For the Human K9Signs, both *sign* and *say* the ***Word.*** I instruct this with sign/say.
- For the Canine K9Signs, you may just *say* (but sign if it helps) the ***Word*** (you need not always *sign* the ***Word***). To remind you of that, I note in the instructions to say/sign with say first. This extra human

movement (signing the dog's sign) can be distracting for some people and dogs. For example, when you are pointing out to your dog that an object is a toy (*That IS Toy*), you would sign and say *That IS,* but only say *Toy. That IS* is the Human K9Sign, but *Toy* is the Canine K9Sign. With practice, this parsing will come naturally to you.

- In some statement lessons (*That, IS, Class,* and *Finish*) your dog should passively observe your signs. Here you may calmly reward your dog if she looks at you or the object, and/or tilts her head (in apparent contemplation). She may be receptively learning the *Word* (the name of the object you are trying to teach her), which you should reward. Rewarding your dog will increase the frequency of the behavior she is performing. The hope is that these behaviors (the visible head tilt and the invisible cognitive learning) occur together, otherwise you'll be rewarding a head tilt alone. It's worth rewarding on the chance the physical and cognitive behaviors occur together.

SIGN: ATTEND

MEANING: *Attend* is a verb, requesting your dog be aware of, and to concentrate on, you or an object/event. Request *Attend* just before teaching your dog something.

GESTURE: Start with your right elbow bent, your forearm out in front, with your right palm down. Make a "V" (victory sign) with your second and third fingers, but with your thumb touching your fourth finger. Sharply twist your wrist so that your palm faces either you (to direct attention to you), or another object (to direct attention to that object). People make this move when they pretend to poke themselves in the eyes.

CORRECT CANINE RESPONSE: Your dog should show pleasant concentration on you or the object.

Sample Lesson

Initially practice in a quiet environment, and use your dog's name to capture her attention. (Read the Canine K9Signs *Name,* beginning on page 178, before trying this lesson.)

1. Place your dog next to you.

2. Sign/say ***Dog's Name Attend***. (For example, ***Chal Attend***.)

3. When your dog looks at your eyes, immediately sign/say ***Yes! Attend,*** and reward with a treat.

Practice Exercises

After your lesson is successful for several days, change step 1 and repeat the above, in the following ways:

- Place your dog farther from you. (Continue with step 2 and 3 above.)

- Start when your dog is looking away from you. (Continue with steps 2 and 3 above.)

- Place your dog in distracting settings. (Continue with steps 2 and 3 above.)

- Change step 3, with your dog attending for longer periods, you delay saying ***Yes!*** then reward.

Tips

If your dog doesn't attend to your eyes, hold a treat in your hand close to your eyes and sign/say ***Attend***. Your dog will look at the treat, and your eyes behind it. After this is successful, don't have the treat in hand as you move your hand toward your eyes. When she attends, sign/say ***Yes! Attend,*** and reward.

Ask for ***Attend*** and expect just an instant of attention to start. As your dog becomes familiar with this request, extend the time you expect an ***Attend.***

Comments

Attend is a critical request, needed for learning. I find it fulfilling to have Chal look at me with full attention, waiting for the next communication.

STATEMENTS:
That, IS, Class, Finish

SIGN: THAT

MEANING: *That* is a pronoun, referring to a specific object mentioned. *That* is used in statements using *That IS Word* and questions *What IS That?*, *What Type IS That?*, and *Who IS That?*

GESTURE: Start with your right arm at your side. Sharply extend your index finger out toward the object of interest. People make this move when pointing at something.

CORRECT CANINE RESPONSE: Your dog should pay attention first to you, then to the object. Your dog's eyes should be focused on and showing interest in the object. Since this is not a request to *Go To,* your dog should not go to the object.

Sample Lesson

With your dog attending to you, do the following:

1. Place an object in front of your dog.
2. Sign/say *That.*
3. Sign/say *Word.*
4. Calmly reward, if your dog notices the object.

Practice Exercises

Throughout the day, do the following:

- Sign/say *That Word* for various objects and events you want your dog to know.
- When approaching a door, sign/say *That Door* (page 161).
- Show a door, then sign/say *That Door.*

Tips

Sign *That Word* before you teach your dog to sign the **Word.** With *That Word* you will have oriented your dog to know you are naming something, preparing her for faster learning. Since this is easy and fun to communicate, use *That* when you or your dog are bored, or stressed.

Comments

Go around naming things, *That IS Door* and *That IS Toy* (page 131). Use the word **IS** as well, you'll learn it as a later option. Reward your dog when she focuses on the named object. She is receptively learning that **Word.** Later she'll be productively learning when you teach her sign *Toy* and **Door.**

See how many times you can use the same *That Word* in one day. Eventually your dog will anticipate that a signing lesson is upcoming on the *That Word.* Using receptive language, you are priming your canine student for future productive language—signing.

SIGN: IS

MEANING: *IS,* a verb, states that one object or word is equal in meaning to another object or word. *IS* helps form statements, such as *That IS Word,* and ask questions, such as *What IS That?* or *Who IS That?*

GESTURE: Start with your right arm at your side, forearm bent up. Sharply extend your pinky finger up, hand closed with the other fingers touching the thumb making a circle. Move your elbow down (pinky up). People make a similar move when pulling a blind or shade down.

CORRECT CANINE RESPONSE: Your dog should pay attention to you and the object, and be ready for receptive language learning. With your repeated use of *IS,* your dog will anticipate an upcoming word and future lesson.

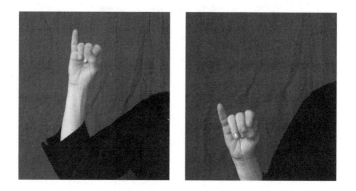

Sample Lesson

With your dog attending, sign/say *That IS Word* in three moves, streamed together:

1. Sign/say *That.*
2. Sign/say *IS,* then pause.
3. Sign/say the new word, *Word.*
   - Replace *Word* with any object name, such as *Toy.*
   - If you find it difficult to say and sign the *Word,* sign and say *That IS,* but only say *Word*—don't sign it.
4. When your dog looks at you or the object in apparent contemplation of the *Word,* calmly reward.

Practice Exercises

Sign/say *That IS Word* for various objects and events you want your dog to someday know or sign.

- When your dog looks at you or the object in apparent contemplation of the *Word,* calmly reward.
- When approaching a door, sign/say *That IS Door.*
- Show a Frisbee, then sign/say *That IS Frisbee* (page 158).
- See how many times you can use the same *IS Word* in one day.
- Sign/say *That IS Word* many times for one object before teaching your dog to sign the *Word* herself.

Tips

Since this is easy and fun, use *IS* when you or your dog are stressed or frustrated with other lessons. On your couch, on a walk or ride, point to objects and say *That IS Toy, That IS Remote, That IS Tree, That IS Truck,* etc.

Comments

With *IS* you are telling, not asking; let your dog calmly reflect and process. This is a receptive language skill, priming your dog for future productive language—signing.

When I sign *IS Word* to Chal, she often tilts her head, looks at the object, turns to look at me with a gleam in her eye. During this silent reflection, we experience a beautiful, bonding moment.

SIGN: FINISHED

MEANING: ***Finished*** is an adjective that indicates that the activity (class, play, food, etc.) is over, done, or gone.

GESTURE: Start with your arms out in front, elbows bent, hands flat, palms toward your body center. Flick your flat hands away from you and out to the side. Show nothing in your hands. People make a similar move when signaling someone to leave.

CORRECT CANINE RESPONSE: Your student should initially be paying attention to you or the object/event. After you sign/say ***Finished,*** your dog should change focus and demeanor, then move attention elsewhere. She may relax, go away, sit down, or even show excitement, hoping for the next activity.

Sample Lesson

Decide what activity or event you want to start, then finish. I'll use play. With your dog attending to you do the following.

1. Lead your dog to a play area, then play.

2. When you are ready to stop playing, say/sign ***Play,*** then sign/say ***Finished.*** (Check the Canine K9Sign Gestuary for ***Play.***)

3. Assume a serious demeanor, then and go into a different area.

Practice Exercises

Many activities (walking, eating, etc.) lend themselves to your signing ***Finished.*** Use ***Finished*** to convey that you are done with the current activity, but you may resume later.

- After you have finished an activity (eating, drinking, going for a walk, etc.), do the following (replacing *Activity* with a particular one):
- Say *Activity,* then sign/say *Finished.*
- Immediately leave the area, then do something different.
- When your bright student learns to sign *Play* or *Food,* she will undoubtedly demonstrate this skill to you (often). Use *Finished* to communicate you temporarily (not forever) are done. This gives your dog hope, yet allows her to learn patience.
- For the first week after you've taught a new sign, when your dog signs to you, respond appropriately (to encourage use).
- After the initial signing period, when you don't want your dog to continue signing (*Play* or *Food*), sign/say *Finished.* Sweetly stop responding (playing or feeding).
- Be sure to resume the activity at a (not too) later time.
- If your dog seems upset and throws a tantrum (after you say *Finished*), don't punish, just leave the room and ignore the behavior. This means she understood! Chal did this just once.

Tips

Even after your dog understands *Finished,* she may continue the signing you don't want. At your discretion, during productive activities (*Class*) say *OK, NOT Finished,* then sign/say *Class* and resume learning activities. Make use of her eagerness to learn more, but change your mind sparingly so as not to dilute the meaning of *Finished.*

Vary what you do after saying *Finished,* so your intelligent canine doesn't think *Finished* means that "thing" you do after finishing (going to your room, putting toys away, etc.) This variation will stimulate your pet to better understand the concept *Finished.*

Comments

Chal has created another sign, I call *Please.* During a naming lesson, I was ready to stop, but she didn't want too. After I signed/said *Finished,* she gently placed her left paw on my arm, looking disappointed. I considered her request, then signed/said *OK, NOT Finished, IS Class.* During the class extension, she learned to discriminate between three different names. Polite negotiation is worthwhile.

SIGN: CLASS

MEANING: *Class* is a noun that defines a lesson, a learning event. In any setting, *Class* creates an expectation of learning.

GESTURE: Start with your arms in front of your waist, palms down and index fingers touching. As you move your hands closer to your waist, turn your palms facing up, and move your hands in opposite directions out to the sides of your body, in a horizontal circle. Your palms will end facing up, near each other, in front of your body. People make this by moving their hands in a big horizontal "C" for Class, starting the "C" center near the belly, and ending the "C" opening in front of the body.

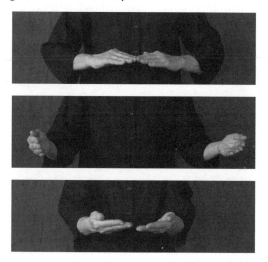

CORRECT CANINE RESPONSE: Your dog should show pleasant anticipation and attention. She may even go to her desk, or the location you regularly learn in. Chal has a low children's desk.

Sample Lesson

Decide what lesson you want to teach or review. Bring your treats, toys, and objects. With your dog attending, do the following:

1. Lead your dog to the classroom area, inside at a low desk or outside in a quiet area.

2. Assume a teacher's presence and sign/say *Class.*

3. Begin your lesson.

4. When you are done, sign/say *Class Finished* to indicate the class is over.

5. Assume a playful demeanor, then go have fun with your dog.

Practice Exercises

After you've had several classes, try this:

- Sign/say *Class* and start to lead your dog to the class area. On the way, wait to see if your dog will lead you to the area.

- If your dog leads you to the class area, say *Yes! Class,* and reward.

Tips

If you find your dog sitting at her desk, she's communicating *Class* to you. Drop what you are doing and start class! Classes should be fun from beginning to end, with plenty of rewards. You want your dog to like class (almost) as much as going out.

As your dog becomes familiar with this sign, she will be increasingly prepared for learning.

Comments

A dog voluntarily sitting at her desk to have class is technically communication, but not yet true language. The reason is that sitting at her desk, she is doing is exactly (not symbolizing) what she wants. If a dog signs *Class* (moving her right front leg in a "C" shape) and then goes to her desk, that would be suggestive of language. Signing a "C" is a learned symbol, having nothing to do with class, until you teach the association. But a dog sitting at a desk is a "class step" in the right direction.

Chal tells me she wants class by sitting at her desk, looking at me. On one occasion, I ignored her request. She persisted, by first nudging me, then as she went back to her desk, she looked expectantly at me to follow. We had class.

While there at her desk, I would sign *IS Word* (*IS Pen*, *IS Cup*, *IS Four*). On a few occasions, where she was having difficulty signing the *Word*, she made up a new sign herself. She'd bend and move her right paw toward me, giving me a look that I interpreted to mean *Teach Me How To Sign It.* How can a teacher refuse that request? I molded her body into the move, and she learned the sign.

FEEDBACK:
Yah . . . Yeah . . . Yes!, Na

SIGN: YAH . . . YEAH . . . YES!

MEANING: *Yah*, *Yeah*, and *Yes!* are adverbs, expressing positive feedback. *Yah* means "close," *Yeah* means "closer" or "almost got it" and *Yes!* means "got it." Sign/say these separately, or together in an extended sequence *Yah . . . Yes!* or *Yah . . . Yeah . . . Yes!* These provide dynamic, guided feedback to your student.

GESTURE: Start *Yes!* with your right hand up in a fist, palm facing forward. Sign by sharply moving your fist down, from the wrist. Nod your head sharply down and up. Sign with only the nod, when your hands are too busy handling a clicker, food, leash, or dog. Say *Yes!* with a sharp positive tone.

Start *Yah* with your right hand up in a fist, palm facing forward. Sign by slowly moving your fist down, from the wrist. Nod your head slowly down and up. Sign with only a slow nod, when your hands are too busy handling a clicker, food, leash, or dog. Say *Yah* (sounds like the Yah in Yahoo) with a tentative but positive tone.

Start *Yeah* just as *Yah,* but the move is slightly faster than *Yah,* but not as fast as *Yes!* Sign by moving your fist down, from the wrist. Nod your head at the same pace, down and up. Sign with only the nod when your hands are too busy handling a clicker, food, leash, or dog. Say *Yeah* (sounds like Yee ahh) with an anticipatory and positive tone.

CORRECT CANINE RESPONSE: After you sign/say *Yah,* your dog should become aware she is on the right track and continue her activity (e.g., lifting the paw, searching the nearby the path). After you encouragingly sign/say *Yeah,* your dog should become aware she is almost there and continue her activity. After you excitedly sign/say **Yes!,** your student should be aware that she succeeded and reached her goal. She'll stop further activity. She should display pleasure, confidence, and an anticipatory look for a reward.

Sample Lesson

For **Yes!,** ask for a simple **Task** in a quiet environment. (**Task** can be any task, but I use **Find** in the example below.) Place your dog next to you, and as she watches, do the following:

1. Toss a treat at your feet.
2. Say **Find.** (If she doesn't know this term, demonstrate for her and tempt her with the treat. Just as your student finds the treat, sign/say **Yes!** (Do this before she eats it, as the feedback is for locating, not eating, the treat.)
3. No additional reward needed.

For **Yah . . . Yes!,** ask for a task such as **Find** that takes a few seconds to perform.

1. Place your dog next to you, and as she watches, toss a treat 10 feet away.
2. Say **Find.**
3. As your dog starts **Find** (heads toward the treat), sign/say **Yah.**
4. As your dog is in the middle of the task **Find** (approaches the treat area), encouragingly sign/say **Yeah.**
5. Just before your dog completes the task **Find** (locates and is next to, not eating, the treat), with excitement sign/say **Yes!** (Give feedback for finding, not eating, the treat.)
6. No additional reward needed.

Practice Exercises

- Ask your dog to lie down, as she starts to lie down, sign/say **Yah.** When she is down completely, sign/say **Yes!**
- Ask your dog to **Find** two treats she saw you throw far away. As she begins the search in the right direction, sign/say **Yah.** When she is very close to the first treat, sign/say **Yeah** enthusiastically. As she locates and approaches the treat (before she eats it), sign/say **Yes!**

emphatically. If she stops searching, encourage her to continue to *Find* the next treat by saying/signing *Yah.* Then repeat the feedback as described here.

Yes! is useful feedback during simple conversations.
- Catch your dog doing something you want to name (*Come, Scratch, Roll*).
- Sign/say *Yes! Word* (*Come, Scratch, Roll*).
- Entice her to repeat the move (repeat the steps).

Tips
Yes! is critical to teach right away, since it helps you teach other gestures and signs. Use *Yes!* to give feedback for all the K9Signs and other behaviors.

Some K9Sign lessons can use guided feedback to teach the gestures. Instead of shaping behavior with only the standard stop and go of *Yes!* or *No,* use guided feedback to guide your dog in one continuous exchange, while she is trying.

Give the feedback quickly (just after a correct response but before the next action), consistently (though intermittently over days, weeks, months). Practice timing the *Yes!* correctly. This is one of the hardest tasks you as a teacher, will have to master.

Don't make a sentence of *Yes!* Your student won't know during what part of the sentence she behaved correctly. But occasionally for special accomplishments, if dog knows what you are *Yessing,* then using a sentence is fine (*Yes! Good Dog, What A Good Job, I'm So Proud Of You*).

After your prize student has mastered a request or task, only occasionally say *Yah . . . Yeah . . . Yes!* and reward. Eventually rarely say *Yah . . . Yes!* and reward. Save that feedback and reward for the new learning. But, as you are rewarding less often for learned tasks, always have new learning tasks in process. Those will involve many rewards. This way your student won't notice (or care as much) that a learned task's feedback and reward are fading.

Common mistakes people make are using variety of words to mean one thing. I've heard people say *Good, Yes, Aha, OK, Awesome, That's Right, Got It* to simply express *Yes!* Keep it simple and swift. *Good* is more general approval of something, not sharp enough for *Yes!* feedback. I will say *Good* to Chal if she is calmly sitting or doing something I like over a period of time. I use *Yes!* if she just did something I want over a short period of time.

Comments

Clickers are valuable because they emit a sharp, short, alerting sound. After conditioning your dog to understand the clicker, she will know when she has performed correctly and will be motivated, as she knows a treat is coming. I highly recommend using this feedback sequence shown below. Notice that the clicker and the *Yes!* are both faded (see page 77).

Perform the sequence in the order presented.

1. First teach the connection between your clicking and a treat appearing. You click, then give your dog a treat.
   Click ‡ Treat.

2. Teach your dog an easy task. When she performs it correctly, sign/say *Yes!* then click, then treat.
   Dog's correct response ‡ *Yes!* ‡ Click ‡ Treat.

3. After many correct trials, sign/say *Yes!* then treat. Fade the Click.
   Dog's correct response ‡ *Yes!* ‡ Treat.

4. After many more correct trials, when she performs the task correctly, sign/say *Yes!* then occasionally, perhaps every fifth try, say *Yes!* and treat.
   Dog's correct response ‡ *Yes!* (occasionally) ‡ Treat

5. After days of your dog performing the task correctly, sign/say *Yes!* but only intermittently after eighth, fifteenth try, say *Yes!*
   Dog's correct response ‡ (intermittently) *Yes!*

6. Occasionally go back to throwing in feedback and a treat. Sign/say *Yes!* then treat.
   Dog's correct response ‡ *Yes!* ‡ Treat.

7. Start teaching a new task (go back to step 2) as you stop giving feedback and/or treats for the first learned task. Keep the treats flowing with new tasks.

Be sure to say *Yes!* before clicking. The clicking will strengthen the impact and meaning of *Yes!* Occasionally recharge the *Yes!* by giving feedback with the *Yes!* ‡ Treat.

Chal and I had fun as she learned how to sign *Ball* with guided feedback. Initially Chal would lift and bend her right front leg. As she moved it, around she'd look at me with an adorable expression, I interpreted to mean *Do I*

Have It Yet? I'd say *Yah* and she would keep moving. I'd point to the left, where she should move her paw. As she slowly moved her paw to the left, I'd say *Yah, Yeah, Yes!* Later when she would position correctly on the first try, I'd sign/say *Yes! Ball.* I love the interactions we have as I teach her and she learns, or at least tries to learn. I hope you, too, experience this same joy.

SIGN: NA

MEANING: *Na* is an adverb that sweetly expresses negative feedback. *Na* means "not quite right, but continue." This provides dynamic, friendly, feedback to your student.

GESTURE: *Na* starts with your right arm bent at the elbow, forearm up, fist forward. Sign by twisting your fist and your head from the side toward your centerline and back. People usually do the head movement when saying *No.* Say *Na* sweetly (with a soft sound) as you sign.

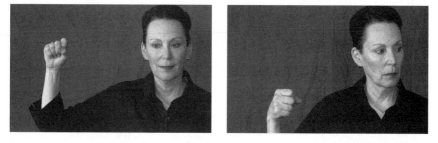

CORRECT CANINE RESPONSE: Your dog should change what she's doing, such as switch directions, try something else, or stop. Your student may look at you for feedback, changing her moves in an effort to get the *Yah* or *Yes!* and the reward.

Sample Lesson

For *Na,* place your dog in a setting she will likely do something you don't want. Present your dog with a temptation (treat or toy).

1. Place a treat by your feet, and sit your dog next to you.
2. As your dog starts to approach the treat, sign/say *Na.*
3. If your dog ceases to approach the treat, pet your dog. If she has trouble holding back, help her resist and gently hold her back.
4. After several seconds of waiting, sign/say *Yes!*
5. Pick up the treat, and give it to your dog.

Practice Exercises

Walk your dog.

- When she moves in the correct direction, sign/say **Yes!**

- When she moves in a direction you don't want, sign/say **Na,** then correct.

- When your dog is not paying attention, throw a treat.

- When she looks at you, pretend to throw a treat in a similar, but not exact, direction.

- If she hasn't already started her search for the treat, tell her to do so.

- As your dog moves in the wrong direction, sign/say **Na.**

- As she corrects herself and moves in the correct direction (help her along), sign/say **Yah** or **Yes!** as appropriate.

Tips

When practicing **Na,** use a task where you can use **Na** to get your dog to behave and later hear a **Yes!**

Pair **Na** with **Yes!** to end with a positive, successful behavior.

Don't get impatient or nag by saying/signing **Na** more than once or twice in a row, if you are not getting a correct response. Nagging is an ineffective method of stopping a behavior. Your dog will habituate to the **Na.**

If your dog is responding by changing behavior with each **Na,** you may say it several times.

Reward after **Yes!,** not after **Na.**

Comments

The sign sequence used together gives elaborate guided feedback on how close your dog is to performing correctly. Steer your dog with the sequence as she tries to achieve the correct behavior. Let's review the meanings.

Na is a nice version of **No** or **Wrong.** No punishment should ever be implied by you or expected by your dog. Use **Na** as feedback.

Yah means "you're getting close."

Yeah is "you're almost there." (You can add this additional feedback.)

Yes! is "that's it."

Use these in succession (***Na, Yah, Yeah, Yes!***) as an animal is trying to do something you want. If you find all four feedback terms too many signs to deal with, just start with ***Na*** and ***Yes!***

But do master them, you'll use them regularly.

REQUESTS:
Try, Freeze, Sign

SIGN: TRY

MEANING: ***Try*** is a verb request (not feedback) that means "keep experimenting, attempting, playing, creating—don't give up."

GESTURE: Start with your right elbow bent, forearm and closed fist facing your centerline. Sign by moving your fist, slightly down and forward. People make this move when holding something (like a vertical rod) and pushing it down, forward, and up. Say ***Try*** with an encouraging demeanor and voice.

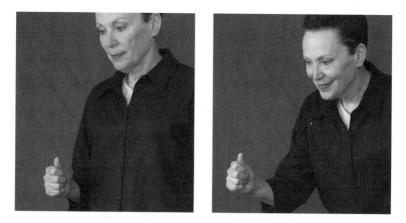

CORRECT CANINE RESPONSE: Your dog should continue to move joyously, in various ways, trying to reach the assigned goal or imminent reward.

Sample Lesson

Give your dog a task she must try for a while before she'll succeed.

1. Put a toy she likes to play with under the couch, just visible.

2. Point to it and say ***Find*** or ***Get.*** (If she doesn't know these terms, demonstrate for her and tempt her with the toy.)

3. As your dog tries to get the toy, cheer her on and sign/say ***Try.***

4. If she keeps trying, reward with a generic treat (from your hand).

5. Finally, when she gets the toy (with your help), say **Yes!** and let her have the toy.

Practice Exercises

Practice saying/signing **Try** when your dog is attentive to you (or can hear you) and trying to doing something.

- While your dog is watching, place a toy or special treat in a room. Don't let her see where in the room you placed it.
- Step out of the room, and say **Find** or **Get.**
- As your dog enters the room to find it, sign/say **Try.**
- As she tries (but hasn't found it yet), reward with a generic treat.
- When she finds it, say **Yes!**
- Let her get her reward (the toy or special treat).
- Place the treat in a hidden location, then repeat the steps above.

Tips

If your dog is having fun trying, give a generic reward; if she is struggling, give her a special reward (to keep her motivation up).

Use **Try** when an animal needs encouragement, while trying to learn a new gesture or task. Be careful to sign/say **Try** just before you give the treat, so your dog associates it with **Try,** not the final gesture. When the new gesture is learned, make it a big event, sign/say **Yes! Word,** and reward with more or better reinforcements.

Sign/say **Try** to inspire your dog to create new gestures while she is communicating.

If you find it too complicated to sign/say **Try** or reward for trying, then just say **Try** and don't reward until the goal is reached.

Comments

Try requires effort, not perfection. Trying itself is worthy of a reward. **Try** and **Yes!** differ. **Yes!** indicates the correctness of the move.

I love to coach Chal with the sign **Try** as she is attempting a new move. After she learned the sign **Animal**, I taught her the sign **Human**, which requires a higher leg lift. As she lifted her leg slightly, I signed/said **Try.** She lifted her leg higher until she signed **Human.** I responded with **Yes! Human** and a hefty reward.

SIGN: FREEZE

MEANING: **Freeze** is a request verb that means "hold your body still in its current position."

GESTURE: Start by bending down toward your dog, right elbow at your waist and forearm out, palm facing down. Gesture by moving your forearm and extended fingers quickly upward, about 45 degrees; then freeze. Say **Freeze.**

CORRECT CANINE RESPONSE: Your dog should immediately stop and freeze its body, mouth, ears, and eyes, looking at you with anticipation. A slightly wagging tail or eye movements are fine initially.

Sample Lessons

When your dog is already holding still (in a **Sit, Down,** or **Stay**), do the following:

1. Sign/say **Freeze.**
2. If your dog stays put, sign/say **Yes!** and reward.

When your dog is slowly walking with you:

1. Suddenly stop (and stop your dog).
2. Sign/say **Freeze.**
3. If your dog stays put, sign/say **Yes! Freeze** and reward.

Practice Exercises

Practice when your dog is tired.

- Ask your dog to *Come.*
- When she arrives sign/say *Freeze.*
- When still, sign/say *Yes!* and reward.

Practice during a chasing game.

- Entice your dog to chase you.
- Then suddenly sign/say *Freeze.*
- When your dog does, sign/say *Yes!* and reward.

Play a game incorporating *Finished.*

- Entice your dog to chase you.
- Then suddenly, sign/say *Freeze.*
- When your dog does, just hold it a bit longer, then sign/say *Finished.*
- Then move around, joyfully playing with your dog.
- No need for another type of reward.

Tips

Teaching *Freeze* is usually successfully done by modeling or imitation. You freeze and your dog duplicates your behavior.

If your dog doesn't freeze her entire body initially, accept that. As you practice, expect and reward more as she freezes more (her tail, eyes, ears). Gradually build to a total freeze.

Try exercises using *What's That?* Say it as though you heard something and want her to listen for it. Chal holds still when I freeze and act as though I'm listening for something.

Comments

Freeze is a useful request for shaping certain behaviors. As your dog is moving and you are giving feedback, when she reaches the desired position, sign/say *Freeze Yes! Word.*

This request is also useful during various activities. At the veterinarian's office, you may want your dog to hold still for a shot or exam. While walking where the footing is risky, on logs, near cliffs, or at the street corner, sign/say *Freeze* to keep your dog safe.

Chal freezes very well when I'm close to her. She will actually stop breathing, freeze her mouth, tongue, eyes, and tail. She particularly enjoys this sign when we are rapidly doing something (fetching, running, chasing, tugging, etc.). The distinct freeze is more obvious (and fun) for her than when we are already standing still.

SIGN: SIGN

MEANING: *Sign* is a verb command, meaning "communicate in a gesture to me."

GESTURE: Start with your right elbow bent, forearm up, hand relaxed. Touch your thumb to your middle finger, index finger pointing to your center line. Gesture by rotating your right hand up and toward you, then down and forward in a circle. Some people make a similar move when saying *Come On.* Say *Sign.*

CORRECT CANINE RESPONSE: Your dog should sign by making a meaningful gesture, not just a trick. The communication can be a natural, made-up, learned, or a K9Sign. If you don't understand the response, your dog could be making up a new sign. Try to figure it out in context.

Sample Lesson

Work with a communication your pet already expresses, such as *Play* or *Go Out.* If you and your dog already have a gesture for "play," skip ahead to page 122 and read the *Play* signing instructions, then go to page 102 for Practice Exercises. If you and your dog don't have a gesture for play, continue with this Sample Lesson.

1. With your dog in a playful mood, lean over in a play-bow (both arms out, head bowing) and say/sign *Play.*

2. While she is looking at you and before she responds, say/sign *Sign Play.*

3. After she responds with a play-bow, sign/say *Yes! Play* and go play.

4. No additional reward needed.

Practice Exercises
- Practice saying/signing *Sign,* just before your dog makes a recogniz-able communicative gesture *Word.* Below, I use *Pick Up* (page 125) or *Scratch* as the *Word.* Sign *Scratch* by scratching with one hand in the palm of the other. Make sure your dog is looking at you, see-ing you sign.

For small dogs:
- Just before your small dog stands up asking to be picked up, say/sign *Sign Pick Up.*
- After she stands up (signs), sign/say *Yes! Pick Up,* and pick her up.
- No additional reward needed.

For all dogs:
- Just before your dog turns her rear to you (to scratch), say/sign *Sign Scratch.*
- After she places herself for scratching, sign/say *Yes! Scratch,* and scratch her.
- You can repeat this many times in one scratch session.
- No additional reward needed.

Tips
Use this sign to request or ask for communication in any form, but especially with the Canine K9Signs your dog will learn in the next section.

When your dog signs to you, respond immediately and appropriately, saying/signing *Yes! Word.*

Pay attention to your own entire body language when you sign/say *Sign.* Your canine student will cue from your unintentional body language as well as from the word *Sign.* Eventually you won't need to request communication with *Sign* because your observant pets will know when they can and cannot communicate.

Very obedient dogs, great learners, initially may be reluctant to learn or even sign. Inspire them by commanding them to sign (after they've learned that concept). To communicate freedom to sign, teach *Sign* while in play or free mode. To promote the potential for language development, your dog needs to sense that you are comfortable with her initiating signing—at acceptable times. In a competition, your dog should not be signing **Food.** Be consistent about when it is acceptable to sign. Dogs do understand the context of when it is acceptable to behave a certain way, sign. Use the sign **Finished** to help communicate when you don't want signing.

Maya, a sweet obedient Labrador, with her person Kelly, attended my CSUMB AnimalSigning class. When we started teaching her to sign for **Food,** she would just sit and look at Kelly, waiting for a command. She hadn't yet learned the request to **Sign** yet. No matter how many times we lifted or tapped her foot, she wouldn't lift it on her own. She was in an obedience mode mind-set. Finally we strategized to teach her during play, where she would naturally lift her leg (and we could get it on cue). On seeing Maya lift her leg during play, Kelly was to label it **Food** and reward with food. She did this by saying/signing **Yes! Food.** Practicing for weeks without obvious results, one day Maya subtly, spontaneously, signed **Food.** From then on, signing has been easier for her. Maya needed to play to learn initial signs, and she needed time to process this new approach to communication.

Comments

Sign is a language request, instructing your student to communicate with gestures. Initially your student can do no wrong, as long as she responds with a gesture. Over time, expect appropriate signing. Your student should feel comfortable attempting movements, gesturing, communicating, and signing. Encourage even if you don't understand the meaning. Your dog may make up signs you haven't learned (from her). Your student may make up a new sign for a special toy rather than sign the general **Toy** word you taught her. (I trust she will use her right front leg.) Watch carefully, for your student might sign something different than what you ask for because she wants to communicate something else. Honor this.

When you don't understand what your dog signs, observe carefully and document. Note what is going on with you, the environment, and your dog. Note your expectations and surprises, as well as persistent or puzzling behaviors. You'll learn to catch signing moments better.

By teaching dogs to expand their natural communication with signing, we are expanding their thought process and developing their communication skills. As pups, they are good at initiating behaviors and communication. As humans, we steered and likely suppressed some communications so our social lives could be manageable. With K9Sign, we are encouraging our dogs to initiate communication but with manners.

When your dog gestures, think beyond obedience (what you want her to do) and ask yourself what she could be trying to communicate. Your signing dog may ignore your requests, and sign something she wants to communicate. Use discretion in your response.

Showing Chal a ball, I asked, **What's That?** She signed **Food**. I was puzzled, so asked again, **What's That?** She signed an exaggerated **Food**. Did she make a mistake? No, she was looking at my bulging treat-filled pocket, and telling me what she wanted. So I pulled out the treats and asked, **What's That?** She rightfully signed **Food** and I gave it to her. Dogs pay attention and learn signs they are interested in, regardless of what we are putting before them.

QUESTIONS:
What?, Type?, Who?

These signs are questions you ask your canine, to which she should respond. **What?** asks for a response about the object/event focused on. **What Type?** asks for a more detailed response about the object/event (type of food or toy).

Who? asks for a learned name (e.g., Michelle, Brad, or Stranger). These questions ask your students to discriminate and respond with an appropriate sign. All questions assist in proofing a student's knowledge of learned signs. After mastery of many signs, use these questions to teach a new sign to a thoughtful student. As you sign/say these words, lift your eyebrows and tilt your head slightly, as you might when asking questions to humans.

SIGN: WHAT?
MEANING: **What?** asks a question about (the name or description of) an object/event.

GESTURE: Start with your right arm at your side, forearm bent up, hand relaxed. Touch your thumb and index finger to form a circle, pinky finger sticking out horizontally. People make this gesture while holding a cup of tea. Sign by sharply flicking your wrist to the side and away from you, end with pinky vertical. Indicate a question by lifting your eyebrows and tilting your head slightly. Say **What?** when signing.

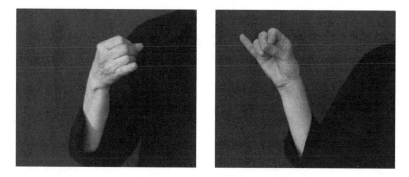

CORRECT CANINE RESPONSE: To respond correctly, your student must know the Canine K9Signs. Your student should pay attention to you or the object, show signs of thinking (head tilt, eyes focused, perhaps slowly moving around), and finally sign appropriately.

Sample Lesson

Before this lesson, your dog should already have mastered K9Signs *Food* or *Toy.* See pages 128 and 131 in the Canine K9Sign Gestuary. Use *What* in combination with *IS* and *That* to make *What IS That?* For short, sign/say *What's That?*

1. Sit your student next to you.
2. Place a generic treat in front of her.
3. Sign/say *What's That?*
4. After your student signs *Food,* sign/say *Yes! Food.*
5. Give her the food.

Practice Exercises

- Sit your student next to you.
- Place a toy in front of her.
- Sign/say *IS Toy.* Pause. (No dog response needed.)
- Ask your student, *What's That?*
- After your student signs *Toy*, sign/say *Yes! Toy.*
- Give her the toy.

Tips

Be calm, friendly, and supportive as your student thinks and responds. Especially with questions, be patient.

Your thinking dog may hesitate, and even pant slightly. This is acceptable, but don't let this develop into an unpleasant, stressful state. If you think stress is building, back up and ask for something your dog will succeed at, as in *Sign Word.*

Help your student learn, make it fun, and use ample rewards.

Comments

What's That? should entice different responses depending on the object of focus. This simple question can help proof your student's skill and test her understanding. Turn this into a fun quiz, not a serious test.

When Chal was a puppy, she would pant while trying to answer a question. I would encourage her, give her hints, and reward trying. Now she enjoys trying to figure out answers. Ears up, tongue out, she looks around, looks at me, tries different answers, usually ending in the correct one (with my help).

SIGN: WHAT TYPE?

MEANING: *What Type?* is a question, asking for a *specific* gesture, describing characteristics of the named object/event. The question asks for more detail than *What?*

GESTURE: Start with your right arm at your side, forearm bent up, hand relaxed. Touch your thumb and index finger to form a circle, pinky finger sticking out horizontally. People make this gesture while holding a cup of tea. Sign by, twice, sharply flicking your wrist to the side, away from you, end with pinky vertical. The first flick is *What,* the second flick means *Type.* Indicate a question by lifting your eyebrows and tilting your head slightly. Say *What Type?*

CORRECT CANINE RESPONSE: To respond correctly, your student must know the Canine K9Signs. Your student should pay attention to you or the object, show signs of thinking (head tilt, eyes focused, perhaps slowly moving around), and finally sign appropriately.

Sample Lesson

Your student should have mastered K9Signs *Food* and (at least one type of *Food*) *Chicken.* (See pages 128 and 143.) Below I combine four words, *What Type IS That?* For short *What Type?*

Teach your student (previously) to sign a type of food, such as chicken.

1. Sit your student next to you.

2. Place a specifically named treat, chicken, in front of her.

3. Sign/say **IS Food.** (No response needed.)

4. Sign/say **What IS That?**

5. After your student signs **Food,** you sign/say **Yes! Food.**

6. Give her the food.

7. Sign/say **IS Food Chicken,** or just **IS Chicken.** (No response needed.)

8. Sign/say **What Type IS That?**

9. After your student signs **Chicken,** you sign/say **Yes! Chicken.**

10. Give her the chicken.

Practice Exercises

Help your hesitant student answer the question with **Chicken.**

- Sit your student next to you.

- Place the chicken in front of her.

- You sign/say **IS Chicken.** Pause.

- Ask your student, **What Type IS That?**

- If your student hesitates too long, encourage by moving her paw and sign/say **Try.**

- As she does try, guide her limb, or make the sign yourself, saying/signing **Yah, Yeah.**

- Finally when she signs correctly, sign/say **Yes! Chicken.**

- Give her the chicken.

Tips

If your dog responds with the general sign **Food** rather than **Chicken**, ask **What IS That?** If she signs **Food** again, reward her. Then ask **What Type IS That?** saying loudly **Type.** Mold your dog's leg to make the **Chicken** sign. Then reward with chicken.

- If your dog is frustrated, return to the general simpler question and response.

Use just the gestures for **What's That?** as you say **What Type IS That?** Skip the **IS.** After much use, you may skip saying **That,** and just sign/say **What?** and point to the object.

Comments

Successful discrimination between general and specific words in the same category, as well as paying attention to the number of times a word (**What, What**) is communicated, represents developing cognitive skills. When your student can do this, celebrate the milestone.

Often Chal just sits by me looking interested in me and what I'm doing. Sometimes I will look back at her and sign/say **What?** Her responses vary. One day she'll sign **Food,** another day **Play** or **Toy.** She's also responded with a backward walk, and muffled bark, to which I say **Show Me.** Sometimes she leads me out to her yard, other times to the biscuit cabinet. If I ask her **What?,** I respectfully respond to her sign. Be careful what you ask!

There have been times where Chal has not responded (to **What?**), instead she would look at me (looking at her); turning her head left, then right. For a brief moment as we "consciously" experience each other, our bond strengthens. These are priceless moments to cherish.

SIGN: WHO?

MEANING: **Who?** is a question, asking for the learned name of someone or some animal.

GESTURE: Start with hand cupped and your right index finger curled pointing toward your mouth. Gesture by moving your hand and index finger clockwise in a circle around your mouth. Raise your eyebrows and turn your head, saying, **Who?**

CORRECT CANINE RESPONSE: Your dog should be looking at your hand near your mouth. When used in conjunction with the sign *That* your dog should next look toward the person or animal you are asking about, or pointing to. Then, she should move her head in the appropriate direction designated as the person's or animal's name. Her head position may not match the person's location.

Sample Lesson

(Read the Canine K9Signs *Name* on page 178 before trying this lesson.)

Teach your student to respond with a particular person's (or animal's) name *Name.* Your student must have already learned the name in her Gestuary.

1. Stand with the person your canine student will name, and your student in front of both of you.
2. Sign/say *Who IS That?* Your student probably won't respond.
3. Say/sign *Name.* When your dog signs *Name* say *Yes!,* and have the named person reward her.
4. Sign/say *Who IS That?*
5. When your dog signs *Name,* say *Yes! Name,* and have the named person reward her.

Practice Exercises

Practice this with several names (already learned), including the student's.

- Stand with the 2 people whose name your canine student knows.
- Sign/say *Who IS That?* (Person1)
- When your dog signs *Name1* say *Yes!*, and have the named Person1 reward her.
- Sign/say *Who IS That?* (Person2)
- When your dog signs *Name2* say *Yes!,* and have the named Person2 reward her.
- Sign/say *Who IS That?* (Point to your dog.)
- When your dog signs (her) *Name,* say *Yes!* and reward her.

Challenge your dog to name someone on the other side of a door.

- Put the person *Name* in front of the door.

- Sign/say **Who's That?** When your dog signs **Name,** say **Yes!** and reward.

- Put the person on the other side of the (slightly closed) door, but still visible to your dog.

- Sign/say **Who's That?**

- When your dog signs **Name,** say **Yes!** and reward.

- With the person on the other side of the door, close the door.

- Sign/say **Who's That?**

- If your dog doesn't respond, either open the door slightly or prompt with **Sign Name**.

- When your dog signs **Name,** say **Yes!** and reward.

After your dog knows the above and can do a **Go To** (go to the person) well, contrast the meaning of **Go To Name** with **Who IS That?** (**Go To** is a request many people use. It simply means you point and your dog goes to where you point. While pointing to her bed, you might say **Go To Your Bed.** Dogs pick this up very quickly. Use the reference training books if you need guidance on that obedience command.)

Ask **Who IS That?**

- When your dog signs the person's **Name,** say **Yes!** and reward.

- Request **Go To Name.**

- When your dog goes to the person named, say **Yes!** and that person should reward her.

Tips

In daily life, for people in the dog's social life, expose your dog to people's and animal's names, saying **IS Name.** Later ask **Who's Name?** or **Who's That?** Answer yourself with **Name.**

Comments

Dogs recognize different people and animals. By teaching your dog how to sign different names, you enable her to express that knowledge. Most dogs easily learn to respond correctly to family name requests. You'll both learn five names in chapter 9, beginning on page 178.

CHAPTER 8

Dogs Can Sign to You

In chapter 7, you learned how to sign the Human K9Signs to your dog. In this chapter, you'll learn the process of teaching your dog to sign Canine K9Sign to you. After studying the information, you'll come to understand the learning stages and terms, and the teaching method for the move and the meaning. Finally, in the next chapter, what you've been preparing for, you'll teach your dog the specific Canine K9Signs that she will sign to you. Doing this will open up a wide range of possibilities for extending your dog's communication capability.

Stages

As your dog learns she will encounter many stages: Moving, Meaning, Trying, Signing, and Creating. Use the different strategies and tools described in this book to pass through each stage. I explain these stages using specific terms in the instructions. I introduced the terms **move, gesture, meaving, and sign** on page 7. Though they are related to signing, each has a distinct emphasis. A move is simply a physical change in a body position. Tricks are made of moves. A gesture refers to a move associated with a meaning (a toy, food, play). This move-to-gesture evolution is an important process I call meaving. When a dog learns a move's meaning, she has meaved the move into a gesture. When a dog uses this new gesture, with apparently intended meaning, or possibly as a symbol representing the meaning, the gesture has evolved into a sign. I use sign liberally, with expectation.

MOVING

First, your canine will need to learn distinct physical moves. This is a procedural skill. Depending on your particular dog's structure and size, moves may be easy or hard. Adjust the move slightly to fit your pet's unique body. The goal is to have your pet make a distinct move, small or large. Dogs can learn the move from watching you, by looking at stick figures or pictures, by your manually moving their bodies, or even by your catching them moving correctly.

Capture and put under cue control as many moves as possible. To do this, entice your dog to make the move and say/sign **Sign Word,** then reward her when she does. These cued moves (tricks) will later be linked to meanings. In other words, the moves will later meave into gestures; and with intended or symbolic use, the gestures will evolve into signs.

Chal has a collection of moves or tricks that have not been meaved into their intended gestures. One such trick is **Scratch,** made with the left hind leg. We meaved it into **Gorilla,** in honor of Koko, the signing gorilla. Chal seemed cautious and puzzled by my having her sign with her left hind leg (living creature) for a toy Gorilla (the best I could do). Toys are movements with the right front leg. A bit stressed, she kept looking around (possibly for the living object associated with this sign). Though Chal will likely not ever meet a gorilla, she will sign **Gorilla** when asked, or when shown a toy gorilla. With toy gorilla in hand, if I ask **What's That?,** she will sign **Toy,** but if I ask **What Type?** she has learned to sign **Gorilla** with the a scratch of the left hind—**Scratch.** Why a scratch? The Gorilla Sign Language for **Gorilla** is pounding the chest, so Chal pounds (scratches) her chest with her leg.

MEANING (GESTURING)

Pairing a move with the object/event's immediate appearance conveys the gesture's meaning to a dog. Start lessons with objects/events that your dog is interested in. (Research by author and psychologist Kathryn Hirsh-Pasek has shown that babies learn to understand words for the objects they are interested in, rather than for the objects their parents and teachers are speaking about.) Your dog will anticipate that gesturing will bring the wanted object. This anticipation helps convey meaning. For example, your dog can learn that a certain move means (results in) food. After your dog gestures, the food appears (and is handed over). When food is already visible and your dog gives the appropriate gesture, she gets the food. Later, when the food is *not* present and your dog gestures, you'll acknowledge her and immediately give the food. Pairing the gesture to the appearance of food as well as to food that is already present helps form the associations needed for language. Take advantage of daily situations to meave moves into gestures. Use what works best.

For some signs, animals may need to learn the move and its meaning separately, for other signs they may be able to learn them at the same time, accidentally or deliberately. To teach the move and meaning together, have the meaning (the object/event) present while you are teaching the move. To teach the move and meaning separately, teach the move, get it under cue control by saying the word meaning as your animal performs the move. Then with the word, ask your companion to perform the move, and then show the meaning. Take advantage of daily situations to meave moves into gestures. Use what works best.

Chal learns best by my displaying the meaning while she is learning the move. She tends to look around to see what the referent object is. She does not seem to like learning just a trick (a move that has no meaning). She is also faster at picking up the meaning of the words I say than she is at learning their moves. Dogs differ; some will learn the trick quickly, and then take time to understand the meaning.

TRYING

Trying refers to your dog's attempts to gesture, either when she isn't certain of the correct movement or when she tests the gesture's meaning by applying it to various objects and events. It is an important stage in learning and should be encouraged. The word is used here as both a noun and a verb.

After your dog can perform the moves with your guidance or under cue control with your request, she will try to test the move on her own. She will try the sign out for this or that, perhaps thinking about what it applies to. She will test whether the sign is relevant in some or all situations. Welcome this exploratory behavior. She's testing the gesture's use and meaning. After she learns **Food,** she'll sign **Food** for everything she wants. She'll try it for **Toy,** for **Pay Attention To Me, Come Hurry, Go Out,** and, of course, **More Food.** Unless you teach otherwise, allowing her to use the sign everywhere will teach her to generalize—the sign means the same thing regardless of where she signs it; it applies everywhere. For the signs in this book, it's safe to allow her to generalize, that is signing **Food** at home means the same thing as signing **Food** in the car. The signs retain their meaning everywhere. (But for some future signs where context helps to define a sign, boundless definition doesn't apply.) Respond appropriately to help your dog distinguish a word's unique meaning everywhere.

A more advanced form of trying will occur when your dog signs at unexpected times (rightly or wrongly so), or offers variations of the sign deliberately. When this happens you must try to interpret what your student is saying. Ask yourself if this is a new variation of the sign (same meaning) or a new sign (new meaning). Encourage the act of trying with the word **Try,** Be sure to reward creative language activity.

On several occasions, Chal has deliberately tried to come up with the correct sign when she wasn't certain. On my presenting her with food she had never seen, I asked **What?** She hesitantly moved her left front leg, up then down, correctly signing **Food,** When I asked **What Type?,** she moved her leg slowly in various ways, looking at me cautiously for feedback. I encouraged her with **Try,** then gave feedback **Yah, Yeah, Yes!** When she made the correct gesture, I signed/said **Yes!,** then treated with that food. She apparently understood the food category, as she used the correct leg for food. And she seemed to understand that she didn't know the sign for that food type. So she turned to me, her teacher, for feedback. With that feedback, we shaped her moves right to the correct sign. Many cognitive processes were involved in this simple interaction—all possible because of the K9Sign groundwork we had already built together. This was fun, fulfilling, and encouraging.

In AnimalSigning class at CSUMB, dogs demonstrate unique and amusing ways of trying. Tobee, a poodle mix, had learned **Food,** but seemed unsure when I asked **What's That?** pointing to the food. He looked away, glancing briefly at the food, his body still. The room was quiet, finally his left paw, ever so slightly, came off the ground. The whole class spontaneously said **Yes!** and he got his earned treat. We all took a moment to pet him. He seemed proud. I wonder if Tobee in turning his head was "pretending" he didn't notice the food, so if he was wrong he could "deny" his move was signing. Luckily he was correct.

SIGNING

After animals have learned a gesture, many will spontaneously use the gesture to communicate or to respond to a question. This is signing. Promote this behavior by enabling your companion animal to control her environment through communication. Dogs will spontaneously sign after learning this gets them something they want. They will generalize the first few learned signs to mean many things. You'll need to steer them to be specific. Watch your dog sign for simple things such as food, toys, and other objects, as well as for more elaborate communication like alerting you to danger, specifically water or stranger.

Signing can influence other communication forms, especially vocalizations. The dog who used to bark for food, can instead quietly sit and sign *Food,* Another dog who endlessly barks to tell you to pick her up, can simply sign *Pick Up,* and quietly achieve the same goal. The more you look for, teach, and respond to signs, the less you might hear vocalizations. You can also enhance communication with shaped and reinforced vocalizations, but that's another book.

My friend Debbie has two gorgeous Yorkies, Taz and Anna Pepper. When they first came over, they vocalized a lot. But after a few signing lessons, they both became calm and quiet around me. I believe they know they can communicate with quiet signs. Taz can communicate *Food* or ask for a *Pick Up* without vocalizing. I listen.

Throughout the book, but especially in the K9Sign Gestuary, I presume dogs are "signing," though I'm fully aware that we do not know what dogs are truly thinking or intending. We can observe their physical behavior in context and interpret as best we can. Surely teaching signing develops canine language and cognitive skills. Even if dogs could not develop true language *naturally,* they might be able to do so with language education. Learning K9Sign Language, especially early in life, might change their brains. To keep expectations high, interpret gestures as signing. This leap of faith emphasizes the intended goal—to teach dogs to communicate with language. At this stage, true language in dogs has not been proven, but this doesn't rule out that, in the future, true language might be proven with signing dogs.

CREATING

After becoming proficient with signs, dogs may experiment by inventing new signs or new combinations of signs. With K9Sign and their natural body language, dogs will have the tools at paw for creating words, phrases, sentences, and possibly true language. True language requires the creative use of existing words and the formation of new word combinations. Dogs will test your response to their creative ventures in order to refine meaning. They might test to see if you agree on the same meaning they proposed. Negotiate and reinforce their efforts.

Consider what your dog might be saying. If you don't understand, keep looking; it may be a new word. Be observant of the behavior and environment, and record in your journal, and review. Remember that observations and interpretations are separate. Your observation of behaviors and events will remain intact, though the interpretation may change over time. This might happen one day when your dog signs something new, which you don't understand. Ignoring it, you later realize she was signing *Potty.* Take notice!

Chal has created (or elaborated with natural signs) specific moves for words that aren't in the Gestuary. When she appears afraid to do something, she communicates *Help* by placing her left front leg snuggly over my arm, then urgently pulling my arm toward her. She has also initiated the communication *Guide* (used when she is not afraid, but isn't successful at doing what I want—that is, she's not getting a treat yet.) To ask for guidance, she moves her bent right front leg (not over my arm) and looks at me in passive anticipation. She uses this often when we are working with numbers or a new difficult sign. To separate this gesture from other signs, I reinforce it, assuring her that I accept her meaning and honor it. I label her gesture with my word *Guide,* get it under cue control, then find ways to have her use it. Your dog may use these specific gestures for other communications. Encourage and label those gestures as new signs.

CHAPTER 9

How to Teach the Canine K9Signs to Your Dog

Your dog is eager to communicate to you. The Model Teaching Instructions explain the basic template; learn and refer to them often. The Canine K9Sign Gestuary of twenty-two signs follows. Each sign includes explanations of the Move and the Meaning, Practice Exercises, Tips, and Comments. The Tips will also note special instructions for special dogs (size, age, temperament, and history). For example, if your dog is small, you may find it easier to teach with your dog on a table at chest level. All dogs should learn all the Basic/Foundation signs, but you should pick and choose what you want your dog to learn from the Intermediate signs. Then, if you'd like to teach her some names and emergency alerts, learn the Advanced signs. Most signs are companion signs, meaning they facilitate bonding and mutual understanding. Other signs are service signs, facilitating mutual care. Teach these signs to your language learner.

The Basic signs teach dogs the concept of extending their gestures to communicate specifically, they teach dogs the easiest signs to learn and represent the general categories of signs for basic body part moves. This learning is easy, fun, and a stepping stone for understanding language. The moves are general (with lots of wiggle room). The concepts of *Food, Toy, Thing,* and

Animal are broad categories for signs within the Basic category. ***Liver, Ball, Car,*** and ***Human*** are more specific Intermediate signs, and the dog's own name is an Advanced sign. Notice that all four legs are used to convey that different body part gestures mean different things. This is something dogs take time understanding, but it is a very important point. Knowing signs for broad categories, dogs can sign to you that something is a food without telling you what kind of food. All these points help dogs develop language.

TIPS FOR HELPING YOUR DOG SIGN

- Promote your dog's interest in using her natural body language to communicate.
- Facilitate dog-useful communications.
- Listen and watch, then respond positively to communication attempts.
- Teach the general Basic/Foundation signs first.
- Then teach Intermediate signs, which are more specific.
- Next teach the Advanced signs.
- Master one sign at a time, and practice regularly.
- Encourage your dog by putting her in situations where she would be inclined to sign.
- Make it necessary and worthwhile for your dog to sign.
- Ignore mistakes or say ***Na.*** Do not use the word ***No.*** (Imagine yourself learning a new language and making mistakes. Hearing ***No*** will inhibit you and stress the teacher-student relationship.)
- Be patient, as your dog may take days to weeks to start signing. Take breaks. Be observant, the signs may appear in a burst, after weeks of "gestating."

K9Sign Model Teaching Instructions

This K9Sign Gestuary begins with model instructions you will implement for each sign. Refer back to this section to review details. Each K9Sign uses the format and system of these instructions. Remember that a **move** is the body position, the **meaning** is the association made to the move, **meaving** these together results in a **gesture.** Then when your dog uses gestures to communicate, they become **signs.** Help your dog develop language skills using these signs.

While teaching, be aware of your body position with respect to your dog. If you demonstrate the sign for your dog to imitate while facing your dog, use the mirror image body part (your left is the dog's right). If you are behind or alongside your canine student (facing the same direction), demonstrate the same body part (your left is your dog's left).

Each sign is taught in four steps:

1. **Teach the Move**

2. **Cue the Move**

3. **Teach the Meaning** in two directions by:
   - linking the gesture to the word meaning (object/event), and
   - linking the word meaning (object/event) to the gesture.

4. **Test the Student** by asking *What?* or *Who IS That?*

Teach the move so your student makes the move on cue. Often the cue will be the spoken word. Teaching the meaning by linking the gesture to the meaning shows your student that gesturing results in the appearance of word meaning (the object/event). Linking the meaning (object/event) to the gesture shows your student that responding to the word meaning (object/event) with the correct gesture results in her getting the object/reward. Testing your student strengthens the gesture-sign connection.

Below I use *Word* to replace the actual gesture word, such as *Toy.* Also, I use object and/or event to refer to the meaning of the word.

Teach the Move: To teach the gesture's move, choose from the many techniques listed below. I refer to "entice" as finding a way to get your dog to make the move. Whatever it takes, do what works. As your dog moves correctly, give guided feedback with appropriate rewards. Use these techniqes to entice the move. When your dog makes the correct move, sign/say **Yes!** and reward. No need to name the move yet.

- Catch your dog making the move on her own. Observe your dog throughout the day, looking for the move you want.

- Shape your dog's moves. Do this in intermediate steps, to reach the final gesture. As your dog makes a partial move (almost there) sign/say **Ya, Yeah, Yes!** and reward. When that move is solid, stop rewarding and guide your dog to the next stage in the move. Reward until you have the final move you want.

- Lure her to maneuver her body. With a treat in hand, move so your dog follows the treat with the appropriate body part to achieve the move you want. Respectfully trick your dog into the move. Use a tool (treat, ball, piece of tape) to structure the move. One trick would be to put tape under your dog's jaw to trick her into moving her paw there to sign **Water.**

- Direct (indicate to) your dog how to move. Direct with your body or with another target object where you want your dog to go, point, or paw. Sometimes just a point in a direction will steer your dog to the correct position.

- Move or mold your dog's body. Sometimes you'll need to actually move and adjust your dog's body into the correct position. At first, your dog may not understand what you want, so be patient. Some students resist having their body molded. With practice and treats, they will learn to relax and let you position them into the correct gesture. Let your students try (and make mistakes) to voluntarily move on their own. But if they try and fail, do not say **No** or **Na,** just quietly steer them into the correct position.

- Use mimicking or imitation. Model the move yourself, or with an assistant, stuffed animal, or sketch. Sign the move yourself; your dog may mimic or imitate you. If your dog doesn't already do this, teach her by practicing the move yourself and then molding her into the move.

- Use the model/rival method. Demonstrate the move with another human (or animal who already knows the move). Ask the person to "be a dog" and make the move you want, then demonstrably reward the person by saying *Yes!,* Good Dog. When your dog pays attention to her rival and wants to participate, teach and praise your dog.

If your dog doesn't respond or move correctly, try something else. Encourage by signing/saying *Try.* Use guided feedback *Na, Yah, Yeah, Yes!.* Try each method from the above list, or use other resources, as needed. For teaching moves, I especially recommend the *The Everything Dog Training and Tricks Book* by Gerilyn Bielakiewicz, Bethany Brown, and Christel Shea. Be creative and resourceful. When your dog makes the correct move, sign/say *Yes! Word.* Your goal is to playfully elicit the move from your student—one way or another!

Cue the Move: After your dog successfully makes the move, get it under cue control. Do this by enticing the move as you sign/say *Sign Word.* Eventually you'll be able to sign/say *Sign Word* and your dog will make the correct move for *Word.* Cueing a move is a trick because it has no meaning. Teaching tricks helps you collect moves for meaving into signs. So practice capturing interesting moves as tricks with cues. Teach meanings later. Some dogs don't need, or like, this cueing step. Many dogs can learn the *Word* meaning while you initially entice the move. Use the process I detail, and as you become skilled, adjust for your dog's inclinations.

Larger dogs may require more effort while learning the move, and might enjoy learning the meaning with the move. Small dogs don't need as much effort to move, so learning moves and tricks are easy.

Teach the Meaning: First, expose your student to the *Word* in context while she is observing and/or gesturing. Sign/say *IS Word* often. Entice your student to move, then make the meaning evident. After the (object/event) meaning appears, entice your student to move. Now you have a gesture. These steps are detailed below.

- **Link the gesture to the object meaning:** With your student attending, entice her to move her body correctly, sign/say *Word.* Then place the object in sight (e.g., make the meaning obvious) and sign/say *Word* again. Remove the object/event from sight and repeat. (Student moves, meaning appears.) Your student will connect the gesture to the *Word* meaning. The move has become a gesture.

- **Link the object meaning to the gesture:** With your student attentive, point to the object/event and sign/say *IS Word.* Entice her to gesture, then reward. Repeat. (Meaning appears, animal gestures.) Your student will connect the (object/event) meaning to the **Word** gesture. Also, the animal will learn that **IS** precedes a word to be learned as a sign.

Test the Student: Ask a question **What?** or **Who?** This tests and reinforces linking the meaning to gesture. Repeat the step that links the object meaning to the gesture (see above), but point to the object/event and sign/say **What's That?** Entice your dog to respond with the correct gesture. Cue your student if needed. Use guided feedback **Na, Yah, Yeah, Yes!** and appropriately reward. Your student's gesture has become a sign of language.

Canine K9Sign Gestuary

The K9Sign Gestuary signs are the future words in your dog's vocabulary. Each sign is listed by level (Basic, Intermediate, and Advanced). With the levels, the signs are further listed by category (actions, food, toys, living, objects, names, etc.). Each sign is divided into similar instruction sections: Sign, Gesture, Teach the Move, Cue the Move, Teach the Meaning, Test the Student, Practice Exercises, Tips, and Comments. First, you teach the move, then get the move on cue with **Sign Word.** Next, you prime your dog with **IS Word** to set its meaning. You test with a question **What?** or **Who?** Finally, you practice with the exercises. Some challenges are predictable, so read the Tips and Comments for guidance and signing stories.

BASIC/FOUNDATION SIGNS:
Play, Pick Up, Food, Toy, Thing, Animal, Potty

SIGN: PLAY

GESTURE: Sign/say the word **Play.** The human move starts in a standing position, hands by your side. Move your upper body forward and down a few inches while extending and slapping your front right arm down enthusiastically. The move is similar to an upper-body and arm stretch down, like a bow, but with energy.

The dog move starts in a stand position. Your dog should move her front torso and extended front leg or legs down, with a pounce. The hind remains up. The move is very similar to a torso stretch or the natural play bow.

Teach the Move:
- Entice the move.
- Catch your dog making the natural move.
- Model the move yourself for your dog to imitate.
- Use other techniques listed in the model instructions (above), as needed.

When accomplished, say/sign ***Yes! Play*** and reward by playing.

CHAL SIGNING PLAY

Cue the Move:
1. Entice the move and sign/say ***Sign Play.***
   - Repeat, until you can sign/say ***Sign Play*** and your dog makes the correct move.
   - Reward this trick with play or another treat.

Teach the Meaning:

MEANING: The sign **Play** can be used as a noun or verb. It names or requests a fun interaction, such as catching a ball, going out to run, or chasing. Your dog probably already knows the gesture meaning.

1. Entice (cue with **Sign Play**) your student to sign **Play.**

2. When she gestures correctly, show the meaning—go play!

3. When your student is playing, sign/say **IS Play** and entice her to sign **Play.**

4. When she gestures correctly, show the meaning—go play!

Test the Student:

When your student is playing, sign/say **What's That?**

1. Entice your student to sign **Play.**

2. Sign **Play** yourself.

3. When your dog gestures correctly, sign/say **Yes! Play** and reward with play.

Practice Exercises

- Start playing ball by yourself (to encourage your dog to sign **Play**).

- When your dog gestures **Play,** sign/say **Yes! Play,** then go play with your dog.

- You can entice your dog to play with you by slapping your hands on your thighs in an energetic manner and say **What?** in a teasing way.

- When your dog gestures **Play,** sign/say **Yes! Play,** then go play.

Tips

If your dog is active and playful, you may need to ask for a **Sit** and **Attend** before teaching signs.

If your dog is very obedient and won't initiate other signs even when asked, put the dog in play mode before teaching a new sign. Practice this request to **Play** before learning another sign. Strengthening the natural play exchange before learning a new sign is a useful tool to help very obedient dogs learn to sign on their own. Be patient; your dog may take longer to initiate signs, but over time she will rise above this challenge.

After learning that the word *Sign* is a request, most obedient dogs do very well.

If you are concerned that once your pet learns to sign *Play* that you'll constantly be playing, deal with this by teaching manners, with the sign *Finished*. If needed, review the Human K9Sign, *Finished* Practice Exercises section on page 87.

During my Canine Wellness with AnimalSign class at CSUMB, we had a very obedient Labrador named Maya. Initially she would not lift her paw, not even for food. Her person, Kelly, would wait for Maya to lift her foot. Maya would just sit, looking at Kelly, waiting for a command. Kelly or I tried to entice her to lift her paw (by gently "stepping" on it) to no avail. Maya wouldn't move. She was a good obedient dog. She didn't know the command *Sign* yet, so we put her into play mode in order to catch her moving her left paw. Once this happened, we were able to label the left leg move as *Food.* Finally Maya learned to sign *Food,* ever so subtly. Later we worked on *Sign Toy* and *Sign Ball,* commands we were sure she would to love to obey.

Comments

Many animals already know how to communicate *Play* to you. As such, *Play* is a convenient gesture to start signing with since it is easy to teach, and it's a clear communication that awaits a response. Use *Play* to strengthen the concept that gesturing is communicating, and that communicating is worthwhile. This word shines a light on the process you are engaging in (with focus) with your dog. Communication channels between you and your dog will open as you both watch and listen for each other's communications and then respond. Your dog will notice this change and surely be delighted.

SIGN: PICK UP

GESTURE: As you sign, say the word *Pick Up.*

The *human* move starts in a standing position, hands by your side. Move your arms forward and up with elbows bent, hands bent at wrists with palms facing the ground. It looks like a begging gesture.

The *dog* move starts from a stand position on all four legs (or a sit position if your dog prefers). The dog should then lift front legs up in a bent "beg" position. Or a dog may jump up and down in a controlled way with the front legs straight if bending them doesn't happen easily.

Teach the Move:

1. Catch your dog making the natural move.

   - Model the move yourself for your dog to imitate.

   - Use other techniques listed in the model instructions, as needed

2. When she does, sign/say *Yes! Pick Up.*

3. Reward by picking her up then giving her a treat.

PICK UP

Cue the Move:

1. Entice the move, then sign/say *Sign Pick Up.*

2. Repeat until you can sign/say *Sign Pick Up* and your dog gestures *Pick Up.*

3. Sign/say *Yes! Pick Up.*

Teach the Meaning:

MEANING: The word *Pick Up* is a verb requesting that you pick up your dog.

1. Entice (cue with *Sign Pick Up*) your student to sign *Pick Up.*

2. When your dog gestures correctly, show the meaning—pick up your dog.

3. As you pick up your pet, sign/say *IS Pick Up.*

Test the Student:

(Perhaps your dog would rather test your understanding.)

1. Sit down with your dog in front of you.

2. Say/sign *Sign Pick Up.*

3. When your dog signs *Pick Up,* say *Show Me* and tap your hands on your lap.

4. When your dog jumps on your lap, hold your dog (as though you just picked her up), and sign/say *Yes! Pick Up.*

Practice Exercises

- When you are going for a walk and you reach a big puddle, or other difficult area, sign/say *Sign Pick Up.*

- When your dog responds by signing *Pick Up,* sign/say *Yes! Pick Up,* then pickup your dog.

Tips

If your dog asks for this too often, sign/say *Finished.* Teaching manners with the sign *Finished.* Review the *Finished* Practice Exercises on page 87.

Taz, a beautiful Yorkie mix, performed many maneuvers to get her person, Debbie, to pick her up. She would beg, spin, bark, and move her paws up and down. I taught Taz to simply do one thing to get picked up—to *Sign Pick Up.* Now she doesn't have to try so hard to communicate.

Comments

Pick Up is a very convenient beginning sign, since it is a clear communication that promotes bonding. As you clarify the gesture and your response, your dog will notice that you are listening.

Teach this sign if your dog is small enough to be picked up safely. Otherwise, skip it, or teach the dog to use it to indicate something else needs to be picked up, such as a ball that needs to be thrown.

Chal knows how to sign *Pick Up,* and also knows not to use it as a request to be picked up. But, one day my horse was stuck in her stall and couldn't get up. This is very dangerous for a 1,000-pound horse. That particular day, Chal's barking wasn't getting the urgency through to me, so Chal performed the Pickup gesture, and I listened. (I listen better now.) She led me to the problem, which I fixed (with much effort). I believe Chal understands she can only gesture that way for a serious emergency, such as Princess or my cats being in danger.

SIGN: FOOD

GESTURE: As you sign, say the word *Food.*

The *human* gesture starts in a stand or sit position hands by your side Move your straight left arm forward and up, to waist level, with palm facing the ground, then down.

The *dog* gesture starts in a sit (or stand) position. Your dog should move her left front leg up, then down, from the shoulder. It is a general move and can be small or large. Specific foods are represented by more precise movements and positions.

CHAL SIGNING FOOD

Teach the Move:

1. Entice your dog to make the move through one of the following methods:

   • Model the move yourself for your dog to imitate. (If you model this gesture facing your dog, use your right arm to mirror what she should do with her left front leg.)

   • Catch your dog making the natural move.

   • Lure, with a generic treat, the left leg into the correct position.

   • Mold, direct, and adjust the leg into the correct position.

   • Use other techniques listed in the model instructions, as needed.

2. When your dog moves correctly, sign/say *Yes! Food* and reward with a generic treat.

   - Do not reward with special foods that you will later name (chicken, liver, cheese, etc).

Cue the Move:

1. Entice the move, then sign/say *Sign Food.*

2. Repeat until you can sign/say *Sign Food,* and your dog then signs *Food.*

3. When she does, sign/say *Yes! Food* then reward with the generic food.

Teach the Meaning:

MEANING: The word *Food* is a noun, an object label that refers to something (not living) your dog could eat.

1. Entice (cue with *Sign Food*) your dog to sign *Food.*

2. When she does, show the meaning by giving her the generic food.

3. When your dog is paying attention to the generic food you put on the floor, sign/say *IS Food.*

Test the Student:

1. When your dog is paying attention to the food on the floor, sign/say *What IS That?*

   - If your student doesn't sign *Food,* prompt your dog to *Sign Food.*

2. When she does, sign/say *Yes! Food* and reward with a generic food treat, but not the food from the floor. This promotes her perceiving food on the floor as the object, distinct from a reward.

Practice Exercises

- Ask her to *Sit,* when she does, say *Good Sit.*
- Show the reward food and ask *What's That's?*
- When your dog signs *Food,* sign/say *Yes! Food* and give it to her.

Repeat the above with other behaviors and games. Before you give the treat, have her name it.

Tips

Be careful not to feed treats with your hand unless you know your dog will not bite or nip you. You can give treats on the floor, from a dish, or throw them.

If your dog already knows the move, then you need only get it on cue and teach the meaning.

If your dog is small, use very small pieces of food, so you can reward often. Adjust meals accordingly.

Comments

The *Food* gesture is relatively easy to teach, as dogs attend to food, and many opportunities exist to teach the sign. The sign is very general, and so is the move. Later you will learn food type signs, where the limb move is precise.

Food has a special role, since it not only the main reward (for some dogs), but also gets named itself specifically. For the general *Food* sign (above) and for most other signs, use a generic food treat, which you will not be specifically naming. It is just *Food.* I use healthy, beef jerky that is easy to break off in little bits with my thumb. For specific food names, you will use those specific foods as the reward. When you teach the word *Chicken,* you will use chicken as the reward.

While teaching other nonfood signs, hide the generic food reward. This will prevent confusion about what you are naming—the generic food or the nonfood. For example, teaching the non-food sign *Door,* have the generic treat reward hidden so she won't think you are asking her to name the treat *Door.* If your dog doesn't want treats but prefers toys as rewards for learning signs, use a generic toy and have that hidden as well.

You may be concerned that if your student learns to request *Food,* you'll be constantly feeding her. Teach manners by communicating using the sign Human K9Sign *Finished.* This enables your eager student to put off gratification. Once she learns the *Food* sign, consistently respond to the communication and feed her. This makes it worthwhile for your dog to sign to you. After a few weeks, as your dog is signing *Food,* occasionally sign back *Finished.* Eventually stop responding to your dog's constant *Food* requests. She may get upset at first, but it will pass (especially if you distract her by smoothly doing something else with her). At the very least, she will understand the meaning of *Finished.*

SIGN: TOY

GESTURE: As you sign, say the word *Toy.*

The *human* gesture starts in either a sit or stand position with arms at the side. Move your straight right arm forward and up to your waist, palms facing the ground, then down from the shoulder.

The *dog* gesture starts in a sit (or stand) position. Your dog should move her right front leg up, then down, from the shoulder. It is a general move and can be small or large.

CHAL SIGNING TOY

Teach the Move:

1. Entice your dog to make the move.
   - Model the move yourself for your dog to imitate. If you model this gesture facing your dog, use the left arm to mirror what she should do with her right front leg.
   - Catch your dog making the natural move.
   - Lure the right leg up with a toy or treat.
   - Use other techniques listed in the model instructions, as needed.
2. When she does this, sign/say **Yes! Toy.**
3. Reward with the toy (or a treat before the toy, if your dog prefers treats).

Cue the Move:

1. Entice the move, then sign/say *Sign Toy.*

2. Repeat until you can sign/say *Sign Toy,* and your dog then gestures *Toy.*

3. Sign/say *Yes! Toy* and reward.

Teach the Meaning:

MEANING: The word *Toy* is a noun, a general object label, which refers to something, relatively small that your dog can handle and play with.

1. Entice (cue with *Sign Toy*) your dog to sign *Toy.*

2. When she does, show the meaning by rewarding her with the toy followed by a treat, if your dog prefers.

3. When your dog is playing with the toy, sign/say *IS Toy.*

Test the Student:

1. When your dog is playing with the toy, sign/say *What's That?*

   • If your student doesn't sign *Toy,* entice (cue with *Sign Toy*).

2. When she signs correctly, sign/say *Yes! Toy* and reward with the toy, followed by a treat.

Practice Exercises

First, practice *Toy* with one toy in one location, then in various locations. Next, practice with a different toy in one location, then in different locations. Finally, play with a group of toys in front of your dog. Let her choose the toy to play with. Perform these exercises following these steps:

   • Say/sign *IS Toy.*

   • Ask your dog to *Sign Toy.* When she does, reward with the toy.

   • Ask your dog *What's That?*

   • When your dog signs *Toy,* sign/say *Yes! Toy* and reward with the toy then a treat.

Tips

Most dogs make this move when playing. You can wait for your dog to make the move herself, then sign/say *Yes! Toy* and reward.

The reward can be the toy itself followed by a treat. Some dogs, like Chal, prefer treats. Other dogs, like Maya, prefer toys as rewards. Use what works. NOTE: If you must use a food reward for a *Toy* sign, show the toy first, then give the treat. If you give the treat first, your dog won't pay attention to the toy.

If your dog doesn't make this move easily, you can lightly tap your foot on your dog's paw; she should lift her limb. Then you say *Sign Toy* and reward.

If your dog doesn't respond, you (or an assistant) can mold her body into the move, then sign/say *Yes! Toy.* Don't say anything if your dog moves incorrectly; just wait, encourage, and help her along with guided practice and feedback. Practice even if you are not seeing an obvious result. Some dogs take a bit longer to process. They will learn it well.

Comments

The *Toy* gesture is relatively easy to teach, as there are many opportunities to do so. When you are about to give or throw a toy, say *IS Toy* or ask *What's That?* The *Toy* sign is very general concept, and so is the move—accept any limb move initially. Later you will teach specific toy signs (ball, Frisbee, etc.) where the same limb moves into a precise position.

Good job! You just taught *Toy* using the model lesson. Your dog learning to gesture *Toy* to you is a milestone. Your dog should know that different leg moves result in different responses from you. Record this in your journal and celebrate—buy each of you a new toy.

SIGN: THING

GESTURE: As you sign, say the word *Thing.*

The *human* gesture starts in stand position, hands by your side. Lift your right foot vertically off the ground a few inches, then lower it.

The *dog* gesture starts in a stand position. Your dog should lift her right hind leg slightly up, then down.

Teach the Move:

1. Entice your dog to make the move.
   - Model the move yourself for your dog to imitate. (If you model this gesture facing your dog, use the left leg to mirror what she should do with her right hind leg.)
2. Catch your dog making the natural move.

3. Gently tap your dog's hind leg.

- Use other techniques listed in the model instructions, as needed.

4. When she does this, sign/say **Yes! Thing** and reward.

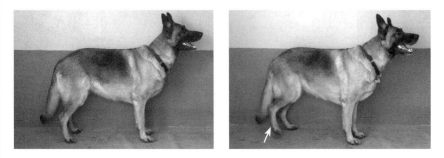

CHAL SIGNING THING

Cue the Move:

1. Entice the move, then sign/say **Sign Thing**.
2. Repeat until you can sign/say **Sign Thing**, and your dog then gestures **Thing**.
3. Sign/say **Yes! Thing** and reward.

Teach the Meaning:

MEANING: **Thing** is a noun, a specific object label, which refers to something, relatively large, that your dog can not handle as a toy. Examples are houses, cars, furniture, bicycles, fences, etc.

1. Entice (cue with **Sign Thing**) your dog to sign **Thing**.
2. When she does, show the meaning by having her interact with the thing.
3. When your dog is attending to the thing, sign/say **IS Thing**.

Test the Student:

1. When your dog is attending to the thing, sign/say **What's That?**
2. If your student doesn't sign **Thing**, entice (cue with **Sign Thing**).
3. When she signs correctly, sign/say **Yes! Thing** and reward with a treat.

Practice Exercises

Interact with the chosen thing, a table, for example.

- Say/sign **IS *Thing,*** as you touch the table.
- Ask your dog to **Sign *Thing.*** When she does, reward with a treat.
- Ask your dog **What's *That?***
- When your dog signs ***Thing,*** sign/say **Yes! *Thing*** and reward.

Interact with a different table in a different room. Follow the same steps as above. Repeat this exercise with a different object, such as the refrigerator. Follow the same steps as above.

Tips

Most dogs make this move often. You can wait for your dog to make the move herself, then sign/say **Yes! *Thing*** and reward.

If you must use a food reward for a ***Thing*** sign, be sure to show, tap, or handle the thing first, then give the treat. If you give the treat first, your dog won't pay attention the thing.

If your dog doesn't make this move easily, you can lightly tap your foot on your dog's paw; she should lift her limb. Then you say **Sign *Thing*** and reward.

Don't say anything if your dog moves incorrectly; just wait, encourage, and help her along with guided practice and feedback. Practice even if you are not seeing an obvious result. Some dogs take a bit longer to process. They will learn it well.

If your dog is not associating the meaning of ***Thing*** with the move, just continue to familiarize your dog with all the parts of the table/thing.

Comments

The ***Thing*** gesture is relatively easy to teach, as there are many opportunities to do so. The meaning is usually the hardest to convey, since the object is large and not as easily focused on. So, for instance, a dog in front of the refrigerator might notice the door rather than the whole fridge.

SIGN: ANIMAL

GESTURE: As you sign, say the word *Animal.*

The *human* gesture starts in stand position. Move your left knee slightly forward and up, then down.

The *dog* gesture starts in a stand position. Your dog should move her left hind leg slightly up, then down.

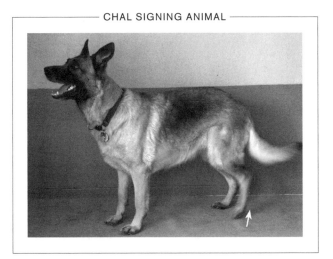

CHAL SIGNING ANIMAL

Teach the Move:

1. Entice your dog to make the move.

   - Model the move yourself for your dog to imitate. (If you model this gesture facing your dog, use the right leg to mirror what she should do with her left hind leg.)

   - Catch your dog making the natural move.

   - Tap your dog's hind leg.

   - Use other techniques listed in the model instructions, as needed.

2. When she does this, sign/say *Yes! Animal* and reward.

Cue the Move:

1. Entice the move, then sign/say *Sign Animal.*

2. Repeat until you can sign/say *Sign Animal,* and your dog then gestures *Animal.*

3. Say/sign *Yes! Animal* and reward.

Teach the Meaning:

MEANING: *Animal* is a noun, a general object label, that refers to a (usually) living animal, including humans. Specific examples are humans, dogs, cats, mice, cattle, and birds.

1. Entice (cue with *Sign Animal*) your dog to sign *Animal.*

2. When she does, show the meaning by having her interact (safely) with the animal.

3. When your dog is attending to the animal, sign/say *IS Animal.*

Test the Student:

1. When your dog is attending to the animal, sign/say *What's That?*

2. If your student doesn't sign *Animal,* entice (cue with *Sign Animal*).

3. When she signs correctly, sign/say *Yes! Animal* and reward with a treat (or appropriate play with that animal).

Practice Exercises

Interact with another dog, for example. Say/sign *IS Animal,* as you touch the other dog.

- Ask your dog to *Sign Animal.* When she does, reward both dogs with a treat.
- Ask your dog *What's That?*
- When your dog signs *Animal,* sign/say *Yes! Animal* and reward.

Next, interact with the same (or another) dog in a different place. Follow the same steps as above. Finally, interact with a group of dogs, preferably at a calm gathering such as a dog class.

- Walk past each dog, enticing your dog to notice each one.
- Say/sign *IS Animal,* as you touch or point to each.
- Go past each dog again, enticing your dog to notice each one.
- Stop by each dog, and ask your dog to *Sign Animal.* When she does, reward with playtime or a treat.
- Go back yet again, past each dog, enticing your dog to notice each one.
- Stop at each dog and ask, *What's That?*
- When your dog signs *Animal,* sign/say *Yes! Animal* and reward with fun playtime or a treat.

Tips

Most dogs make this move often. You can wait for your dog to make the move herself, then sign/say *Yes! Animal* and reward.

If you must use a food reward (instead of just interaction) for the *Animal* sign, be sure to show, touch, point to the person before giving the treat. You or the person may give the treat. If you give the treat first, your dog won't pay attention the person as much.

If your dog doesn't make this move easily, you can lightly tap your foot on your dog's paw; she should lift her limb. Then you say *Sign Animal* and reward.

If your dog moves incorrectly, just wait, encourage, and help her along with guided practice and feedback.

If your dog is not associating the meaning of *Animal* with the move, just continue to familiarize your dog with *Animal* by saying *IS Animal* often. Use it when someone is at the door, when your dog is interested in a guest, when you come home. Don't forget that you, too, are an animal and can point to yourself while saying *IS Animal* or *What's That?*

Comments

The *Animal* gesture is relatively easy to teach, as there are many opportunities to do so. The meaning is usually the hardest to convey, since the object is often large. A dog standing in front of a person may think you are referring to only a part of the human (perhaps a treat in their pocket) rather than the whole human or large animal. Small animals can be easier to notice, but may not be as available as large humans for practice. Later your canine will learn a specific type of *Animal* called *Human.*

Search and rescue (SAR) dogs might be interested in these signs (in addition to *Dead* and *Alive*), to specifically identify the found animal type (human, dog, cat, deer, cat, bird, etc.) and condition (living or dead).

SIGN: POTTY

GESTURE: As you sign, say **Potty.** Three easy optional signs are explained.

The *human* gesture starts in a standing position, hands by your side. Move your legs out in a wide stance, or spin your body in a circle, or ring a special bell.

The *dog* gesture starts in a stand position. Your dog should do one of the following three popular signs: 1) back legs form a wide stance, with or without a crouch, or 2) spin in circles, or 3) ring a special bell. Pick the one that is easiest for your dog and one that your dog doesn't already do often. The instructions below are for the wide stance, but replace with the other sign options as appropriate.

CHAL SIGNING POTTY

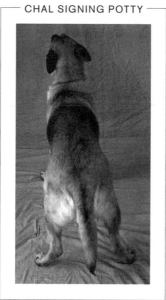

Teach the Move:

1. Entice your dog to make the move.

    - If you model this move, stand with your legs next to your dog's hind legs.

    - Catch your dog making the natural move (before she actually goes potty).

    - Place an object your dog can straddle, and guide your dog to walk "over" it (no jumping).

    - Physically mold your dog's legs into position. First one leg, then the other.

2. Use other techniques listed in the model instructions, as needed.

3. When she does this, sign/say *Yes! Potty* and give a treat.

Cue the Move:
1. Entice the move, then sign/say *Sign Potty.*
2. Repeat until you can sign/say *Sign Potty,* and your dog signs *Potty.*
3. Say/sign *Yes! Potty,* then reward with a generic treat.

Teach the Meaning:
MEANING: *Potty* is a noun or verb. *Potty* alone means a potty area, or the potty substance—poop, a noun. *Go Potty,* means go ahead and do it! Saying *Sign Potty* to your dog means "sign to me that you need to go to the potty area." You can also have your dog identify the poop as *Potty.* Use the sign either way, whichever is useful.

1. Place yourself and your dog by the usual potty area.
2. Entice (cue with *Sign Potty*) your dog to sign *Potty.*
3. When she does, say *Yes! Potty* and reward.
4. As your dog is looking at the potty area, sign/say *IS Potty.*
5. Walk your dog into the potty area.
6. Say/sign *Go Potty Here,* or *Go Potty Now* (while you make the gesture yourself).
7. When she does go potty, though it is its own reward, praise and treat her.

Test the Student:
Test that your dog understands the gesture by doing the following:
1. With your dog by the potty area, sign/say *What's That?*
2. When your dog signs *Potty,* sign/say *Yes! Potty* and reward with a treat.
3. When your dog is about to *Go Potty,* ask *What's That?*
4. If she signs *Potty,* sign/say *Yes! Go Potty Here* and let her do it in peace.

(If the last two steps are too disruptive for your dog, skip them.)

Practice Exercises

Practice *Potty* in specific potty locations.

- When passing a special potty area, sign/say *IS Potty.*
- As your dog is looking at it, or more likely smelling it, request her to *Sign Potty.*
- When she does, sign/say *Yes! Potty* and reward with a long smell of the area.
- With your dog by various potty areas, sign/say *What's That?*
- When your dog signs *Potty,* sign/say *Yes! Potty* and reward with a treat or long smell time.

If your dog signs *Potty,* do the following:

- Say *I Get It, Potty. OK.*
- Immediately take your dog to the potty area.
- Say/sign *Go Potty, Here* (or *Now*).
- When she's done, ask her *What's That?*
- When your dog signs *Potty,* sign/say *Yes! Potty* and reward with a treat.

Tips

If your dog already nudges or goes to the door for this, it should be easy to replace the nudge with this gesture before taking your dog to the potty area.

If you travel often, using wide stance won't work for you in the car. Use one of the other gestures that she can do in the car: ring a special bell that you have placed in the car, use a certain bark you reinforced, a specific squeaky toy with a special sound. Every time she communicates *Potty* in the car, you take her to go potty. Another option is to teach her to make a unique move in the car such as placing both paws on the top of the front seat (only if she is in the back and doesn't usually do that behavior).

Comments

It is very useful for animals to learn to communicate and distinguish *Potty* from *Go Out.* Your behavior in responding to the communication must differ. When your dog signs *Potty,* respond in one way—take her out to the potty area. Teach her that to simply **Go Out** requires a different sign—she goes out but not to potty (at least not for a while).

Many people use or recognize a **Potty** sign. Chal doesn't use it, as she has her special door to go out when we are home. In the car, she never shows signs of needing to potty (and we stop often). On future trips we'll be reviewing the sign, in case she ever needs to tell me. But a puppy could benefit from the sign.

This is a good example that demonstrates the difference between communication and formal language. If your animal goes up to you, starts the move she'd normally do to go potty (but doesn't go) as an indication she needs to go, this is considered communication. But if she learns to bring you a special object, to indicate she needs to go potty, that is more like language. Bringing the object has nothing innately to do with potty, until it is learned as a sign.

Dogs can, on their own, use natural gestures to communicate. Humans smart enough to notice can tweak and/or reinforce these communications by incorporating these natural gestures into the dog's growing K9Sign vocabulary. Perceptive and smart dogs can mediate between less literate dogs and their humans.

Harold tried to teach Maria, a deaf Border collie, to ring a bell to mean **Potty.** She instead attributed a different meaning to the bell. She'd ring the bell to apparently prompt her gatekeeper to jump up to open the door, as she sat watching and staying inside. At four months, Maria learned that if she poked Harold with her paw, backed away about three feet, then calmly crouched (to demonstrate the act of pooping without doing so), he'd let her out to go **Potty.** Harold's keen observation of, and response to, Maria's first deliberate use of the K9Sign for **Potty,** facilitated incorporating this word into her vocabulary.

A typical Border collie, Maria loves to watch animals outside through a glass patio door. She barks when other creatures enter her yard, but also barks when she needs to go out to potty. Unfortunately Maria sometimes fails to communicate her need until it's a crisis. With Maria barking at various times for various reasons, Harold occasionally doesn't hear or recognize her **Potty** bark. But her mother, Lace, never misses the specific communication. Lace has helped her daughter, Maria, convey this message by alerting Harold to her need. Lace finds Harold, then while staring at him, she vigorously nudges his arm, leads and pushes him along to Maria who is waiting anxiously at the door.

INTERMEDIATE SIGNS:
Chicken, Liver, Cheese, Water, Ball, Frisbee, Door, Phone, Car, Human

Teach these signs after you and your canine student have mastered the Basic/Foundation signs. The intermediate signs are specific types of the general Basic/Foundation signs.

SIGN: CHICKEN

GESTURE: As you sign, say the word ***Chicken.***

The *human* gesture starts in a sit or stand position, hands by your side. Move your straight, left arm, forward and up high above your shoulder, then down to your side again.

The *dog* gesture starts in a sit (or stand) position. Your dog should move her straight, left front leg, up high above the shoulder, then down. This is a specific movement.

CHAL SIGNING CHICKEN

Teach the Move:

1. Entice your dog to make the move.

   • Model the move yourself for your dog to imitate. (If you model this gesture facing your dog, use your right arm to mirror what she should do with her left front leg.)

- Catch your dog making the natural move.
- Lure the leg up with a piece of chicken.
- Mold, direct, and adjust the leg into correct position.
- Use other techniques listed in the model instructions, as needed.

2. When she does this, sign/say **Yes! Chicken** and reward with (dried or wet) chicken.

Cue the Move:

1. Entice the move, then sign/say **Sign Chicken.**
2. Repeat until you can sign/say **Sign Chicken,** and your dog signs **Chicken.**
3. Say/sign **Yes! Chicken,** then reward with chicken.

Teach the Meaning:

MEANING: **Chicken** is a noun, referring to a *specific* food type. It is also a **Food** word.

1. Entice (cue with **Sign Food**) your dog to sign **Food.** When she does, show the food meaning by giving her a small piece of chicken.
2. Put the chicken in front of your dog. When she looks at it, sign/say **IS Food.**
3. Entice (cue with **Sign Chicken**) your dog to sign **Chicken.** When she does, show the meaning by giving her a larger piece of chicken.
4. Put some chicken in front of your dog. When she looks at it, sign/say **IS Chicken** (or **IS Food Chicken**).

Test the Student:

1. When your dog is looking at the chicken, sign/say **What's That?**
2. When she signs **Food,** sign/say **Yes! Food** and reward with the chicken.
3. When your dog is looking at the chicken, sign/say **What Type IS That?**
4. If your student doesn't sign **Chicken,** tell your dog to **Sign Chicken.**
5. When she does, sign/say **Yes! Chicken** and give her a big piece of chicken.

Practice Exercises

Practice ***Chicken*** in various locations. Perform these exercises in order. With your dog watching, place a piece of chicken on top of a pillow.

- Say/sign ***What Type IS That?***
- When your dog signs ***Chicken,*** sign/say ***Yes! Chicken*** and give it to her.

With your dog watching, place a piece of chicken under the pillow.

- Say/sign ***What Type IS That?*** Point to the area under the pillow.
- When your dog signs ***Chicken,*** sign/say ***Yes! Chicken*** and give it to her.

After asking for difficult responses from your dog, just before you reward with chicken, do the following:

- Ask her ***What's That?***
- If your dog signs ***Food,*** sign/say ***Yes! Food*** and give a small piece to her.
- Ask her ***What Type IS That?***
- When your dog signs ***Chicken,*** sign/say ***Yes! Chicken*** and give the large piece to her.

Tips

Master ***Food*** before attempting ***Chicken.*** When teaching or asking for specific food signs, ask ***What's That?*** (food), then ask ***What Type IS That?*** (chicken). With practice, you'll be able to drop the ***What's That?*** and just ask ***What Type IS That?***

If your dog signs ***Food*** instead of ***Chicken,*** use the ***Yah*** (not ***Yes!***) to indicate she is close to the sign. Do not use ***No*** or ***Na.*** (Chal understood that distinction quickly and clearly.)

If your dog is persistently confused about the difference between ***Food*** and ***Chicken,*** then skip the ***What Type IS That?*** for a month. During that time, strengthen the ***Food*** and other general gestures. Learn other words in broad categories, not types.

Comments

This is a specific *type* of food sign. The ***Food*** gesture is relatively easy to teach, but the ***Chicken*** or other food *types* can be harder for some dogs. Be patient. Make sure your dog understands or uses the ***Food*** gesture consistently for days before teaching the specific signs.

Your dog learning ***Food*** and specific signs, such as ***Chicken,*** is significant. She knows that movements from different legs result in different responses from you. She also knows that different movements from the same limb provoke other responses from you. Using these different gestures increases your dog's vocabulary and ability to communicate specifically.

SIGN: LIVER

GESTURE: As you sign, say the word ***Liver.***

The *human* gesture starts in a standing position, hand at the side. Move your bent left arm, with limp wrist, in close to your chest center.

The *dog* gesture starts in a sit position. Your dog should move her bent left front leg, in close to her center chest. This is a specific movement.

Teach the Move:

1. Entice your dog to make the move.

   • Mold, direct, and adjust the leg into correct position. (If you model this gesture facing your dog, use your right arm to mirror what she should do with her left front leg.)

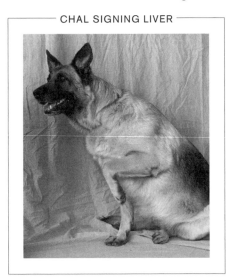

CHAL SIGNING LIVER

- Catch your dog making the natural move.
- Lure the leg into the correct position with a treat.
- Use other techniques listed in the model instructions, as needed.

2. When she does this, sign/say *Yes! Liver* and reward with liver.

Cue the Move:

1. Entice the move, then sign/say *Sign Liver.*
2. Repeat until you can sign/say *Sign Liver* and your dog signs *Liver.*
3. Say/sign *Yes! Liver,* and reward with liver.

Teach the Meaning:

MEANING: *Liver* is a noun, referring to a *specific* food type.

1. Entice (cue with *Sign Food*) your dog to sign *Food.* When she does, show the food liver meaning by giving her a small piece of liver.
2. Put some liver in front of your dog. When she looks at it, sign/say *IS Food.*
3. Entice (cue with *Sign Liver*) your dog to sign *Liver.* When she does, show the meaning by giving her a larger piece of liver.
4. Put some liver in front of your dog. When she looks at it, sign/say *IS Liver* (or *IS Food Liver*).

Test the Student:

1. When your dog is looking at the liver, sign/say *What's That?*
2. When she signs *Food,* sign/say *Yes! Food* and reward with a small piece of liver.
3. When your dog is looking at the liver, sign/say *What Type IS That?*
4. If your student doesn't sign *Liver,* tell your dog to *Sign Liver.*
5. When she does, sign/say *Yes! Liver* and give her a *big* piece of liver.

Practice Exercises

Practice *Liver* in various locations. Perform these exercises in order.
With your dog watching, place a piece of liver on *top* of a pillow.

- Say/sign *What Type IS That?*
- When your dog signs *Liver,* sign/say *Yes! Liver* and give it to her.

With your dog watching, place a piece of liver *under* the pillow.

- Say/sign **What Type IS That?** Point to the area under the pillow.
- When your dog signs **Liver,** sign/say **Yes! Liver** and give it to her.

Ask for difficult tasks from your dog, but just before you reward with liver, do the following:

- Ask her **What's That?**
- If your dog signs **Food,** sign/say **Yes! Food** and give a small piece to her.
- Ask her **What Type IS That?**
- When your dog signs **Liver,** sign/say **Yes! Liver** and give the large piece to her.

Tips

Teach **Food** before teaching **Liver.** If, when you ask for **Liver,** your dog signs **Food,** use guided feedback (**Yah** to **Yes!**) to shape the gesture. Do not use **No** or **Na.** Adjust the leg position by slowly pushing the leg in toward her chest. Use **Freeze** to instruct her to hold the correct position. When correct, sign/say feedback **Yes! Liver.**

If your dog signs **Food** instead of **Liver,** use the **Yah** or **Yeah** (not **Yes!**) to indicate she is close to the sign. Do not use **No** or **Na.**

If your dog is persistently confused about the difference between **Food** and **Liver,** then skip the **What Type IS That?** for a while. During that time, work on **Food** and other gestures. Learn other words in broad categories rather than types.

When asking for specific food signs, ask **What's That?** (food), then ask **What Type IS That?** (liver). Over time, you'll be able to drop the **What's That?** and just ask **What Type IS That?**

Comments

This is a specific *type* of food sign. The **Food** gesture is relatively easy to teach, but the food *types* can be harder for some dogs. Be patient.

Your dog learning **Food** and **Liver** is significant. She knows that movements from different legs result in different responses from you, but also that different movements from the same limb also provoke other responses from you. Using these different gestures enhances her vocabulary and communication skills. She will take advantage of this soon.

Chal understood the distinction between these signs quickly and clearly. Chal first attempted this sign by bending her left leg. I gave her feedback with **Yah.** Then I just lightly pushed my finger into her leg. She moved her leg close to her chest (the correct position). I said **Freeze.** She held the correct position. I said **Yes! Liver** and gave her the liver.

SIGN: CHEESE

GESTURE: As you sign, say the word **Cheese.**

The *human* gesture starts in a standing position, hands by your side. Move your left forearm up in front of your body, to waist level, with a limp wrist, palm facing the ground.

The *dog* gesture starts in a sit position. Your dog should move her bent left front leg, directly in front of her shoulder. This is a specific movement.

Teach the Move:

1. Entice your dog to make the move.

   • Mold, direct, and adjust the leg into correct position. (If you model this gesture facing your dog, use your right arm to mirror what she should do with her left front leg.)

   • Catch your dog making the natural move.

CHAL SIGNING CHEESE

- Lure the leg into the correct position with a toy or treat.
- Use other techniques listed in the model instructions, as needed.

2. When she does this, sign/say **Yes! Cheese** and reward with cheese.

Cue the Move:

1. Entice the move, then sign/say **Sign Cheese.**
2. Repeat until you can sign/say **Sign Cheese** and your dog signs **Cheese.**
3. Say/sign **Yes! Cheese,** then reward with cheese.

Teach the Meaning:

MEANING: **Cheese** is a noun, referring to a *specific* food type. It is also a **Food** word.

1. Entice (cue with **Sign Food**) your dog to sign **Food.** When she does, show the food cheese meaning by giving her a *small* piece of cheese.
2. Put some cheese in front of your dog. When she looks at it, sign/say **IS Food.**
3. Entice (cue with **Sign Cheese**) your dog to sign **Cheese.** When she does, show the meaning by giving her a *big* piece of cheese.
4. Put some cheese in front of your dog. When she looks at it, sign/say **IS Cheese** (or **IS Food Cheese**).

Test the Student:

1. When your dog is looking at the cheese, sign/say **What's That?**
2. When she signs **Food,** sign/say **Yes! Food** and reward with a small piece of cheese.
3. When your dog is looking at the cheese, sign/say **What Type IS That?**
4. If your student doesn't sign **Cheese,** tell your dog to **Sign Cheese.**
5. When she does, sign/say **Yes! Cheese** and give her a *big* piece of cheese.

Practice Exercises

Practice *Cheese* in various locations. Perform these exercises in order. With your dog watching, place a piece of cheese on top of a pillow.

- Say/sign *What Type IS That?*
- When your dog signs *Cheese,* sign/say *Yes! Cheese* and give it to her.

With your dog watching, place a piece of cheese under the pillow.

- Say/sign *What Type IS That?* Point to the area under the pillow.
- When your dog signs *Cheese,* sign/say *Yes! Cheese* and give it to her.

Ask for difficult tasks from your dog, but just before you reward with cheese, do the following:

- Ask her *What's That?*
- If your dog signs *Food,* sign/say *Yes! Food* and give a small piece to her.
- Ask her *What Type IS That?*
- When your dog signs *Cheese,* sign/say *Yes! Cheese* and give a large piece to her.

Tips

Master *Food* before attempting *Cheese.* When you ask for *Cheese,* if your dog signs *Food,* use guided feedback (*Yah* to *Yes!*) to shape the gesture. Don't use *Na* or *No.* Manually adjust her leg position. Use *Freeze* to instruct her to hold the correct position. Then sign/say feedback *Yes! Cheese.*

If your dog is persistently confused about the difference between *Food* and *Cheese,* then skip the *What Type IS That?* for a while. During that time, work on *Food* and other gestures. Learn other words in broad categories rather than types.

Chal made the move on her own, I told her to *Freeze.* She did. I said, *Yes! Cheese,* and gave her the cheese.

Comments

The *Food* gesture is relatively easy to teach, but the *Cheese* or other food *types* can be harder for some dogs.

When teaching or asking for specific food signs, ask *What's That?* (food), then ask *What Type IS That?* (cheese). Over time, you'll be able to drop the *What's That?* and just ask *What Type IS That?*

Your dog learning **Food** and **Cheese** is significant. She knows that movements from different legs result in different responses from you. She also knows that different movements from the same limb also provoke other responses from you. She has more words to communicate with, and she will take advantage of this soon.

SIGN: WATER

GESTURE: As you sign, say the word **Water.**

The *human* gesture starts in a standing position, hands by your side. Move your left hand (palm facing toward you) to your chin. If you teach this gesture facing your dog, use the other arm to mirror what she should do.

The *dog* gesture starts in a stand position. Your dog should move her left front leg up, so that her paw touches her left mouth (lower jaw). This is a specific movement, similar to **Food,** but requires touching the side of the mouth, and holding.

CHAL SIGNING WATER

Teach the Move:

1. Entice your dog to make the move.

   - If you model this gesture facing your dog, use your right arm to mirror what she should do with her left front leg. Catch your dog making the natural move.

   - Lure the leg and paw to her jaw (where your hand has a treat).

- Mold, direct, and adjust to achieve the correct *Water* move.
- Use other techniques listed in the model instructions, as needed.

2. When she does this, sign/say *Yes! Water* and drop a generic treat in water for her to eat.

Cue the Move:

1. Entice the move, then sign/say *Sign Water.*
2. Repeat until you can sign/say *Sign Water* and your dog signs *Water.*
3. Say/sign *Yes! Water,* then reward with a generic treat in water.

Teach the Meaning:

MEANING: *Water* is a noun, which refers to a liquid "food." *Water* is unique as a left front leg sign, and we don't ask for the *Food* type response.

1. Entice (cue with *Sign Water*) your dog to sign *Water.*
2. When she does, show the meaning by giving her a generic treat just dropped in a water dish.
3. Put this water dish in front of your dog.
4. When she looks at it, sign/say *IS Water.*

Test the Student:

1. When your dog is looking at the water dish, sign/say *What's That?*
2. When she signs *Water,* say *Yes! Water* and reward with the generic treat dropped in water.

Practice Exercises

Practice *Water* initially when your dog is thirsty. Use generic treats. With your dog watching, place a water dish in front of her.

- Splash the water, while signing/saying *IS Water.*
- Say/sign *Sign Water.* When she does, say *Yes! Water* and reward with a treat dropped in water.
- Say/sign *What's That?*
- When your dog signs *Water,* sign/say *Yes! Water* and reward with the treat in water.
- Show her the generic treat, ask *What's That?*

- When your dog signs *Food,* sign/say *Yes! Food* and reward with the dry treat.

When your dog is thirsty and drinking, do the following, only if your dog doesn't get upset.

- Gently move the dish slightly away from her (so she stops drinking).
- Ask her *What's That?*
- When your dog signs *Water,* sign/say *Yes! Water* and return the water dish to her.
- Let her drink a few seconds.
- Repeat steps again.

Hold the left paw up to touch the jaw, or use a target on the lower chin for your dog to follow with its paw, or other method, to make your student touch its chin with its paw. Then say/sign *Water.* Reward with the water-dipped generic treat. Or you can drop the treat in the water bowl for the dog to get.

Tips
Teach this gesture after your dog can perform *Food* consistently for days. If your dog has trouble making the move correctly, try the following:

- Place the water dish in front of her, have some thick transparent or masking tape and be ready for quick action.
- Place a piece of tape under her left jaw.
- As your dog tries to take the tape off with her left paw, say/sign *Yes! Water* and reward with a watered treat. Remove the tape so your dog doesn't eat it.
- Using the clicker after you say *Yes!* makes this easy.
- Repeat these steps several times.
- Go back up to Cue the Move, Teach the Meaning, and finally, Test the Student.

If your dog doesn't get the move and meaning, stop teaching *Water* for a month or so. Continue to label water, by signing/saying *IS Water.*

Comments

The ***Water*** gesture is not as common as other gestures and it is slightly harder to perform. However, there are many opportunities to teach it, as dogs drink often.

This gesture is useful for animals to indicate thirst, especially if in a car, at a sport or search event, or at any location where they can't access water. Your dog may already have body language that communicates thirst, but teaching the K9Sign extends the clarity of communication to you. You may already know the signs of thirst in your dog. Now your dog can tell you early on, and she is not dependent on your late perceptions.

If your dog asks for water too often (or urinates too often), you might want to bring her to her veteranarian. In humans, those can be signs of diabetes.

Chal has used the ***Water*** sign on her own to communicate to me she needed water. I was on the couch watching TV, when she came over, looked at me, and signed ***Water.*** I paused (very excited about this). To check her motivation, I asked ***Show Me.*** She walked over to her water dish, which was empty. I said ***Good Girl, Chal Wants Water. Let's Get Water*** (as I walked to the sink). As I filled her dish, I said/signed ***I Get Water.*** As I placed the water dish in her area, I said/signed ***Here IS Water.*** I asked her ***What's That?*** She signed ***Water.*** I left her alone to drink.

One client dog learned to sign ***Water*** by molding, simply moving the paw to the chin, and saying ***Water;*** another dog was irritated by the tape, so we used food stuck to the lower jaw, which worked; most do well with tape. Be sure to remove the tape so your dog doesn't eat it.

SIGN: BALL

GESTURE: As you sign, say the word ***Ball.***

The *human* gesture starts in a sit or stand position, hands by your side. Move your bent right arm, toward your left side, but not near your body.

The dog gesture starts in a sit (or stand) position. Your dog should move her bent right front leg toward her left side, but not near her body. This is a specific movement.

Teach the Move:

1. Entice your dog to make the move.

   - If you model this gesture facing your dog, use your left arm to mirror what she should do with her right front leg.

- Mold, direct, and adjust the right leg.
- Lure the leg movement with a toy or treat.
- Catch your dog making the natural move.
- Use other techniques listed in the model instructions, as needed.

2. When she does this, sign/say *Yes! Ball.*
3. Reward with the ball (and a treat if needed).

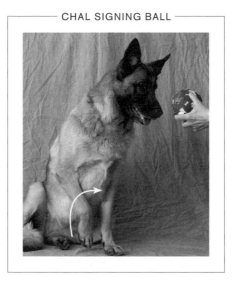

CHAL SIGNING BALL

Cue the Move:

1. Entice the move, then sign/say *Sign Ball.*
2. Repeat until you can sign/say *Sign Ball* and your dog signs *Ball.*
3. Say/sign *Yes! Ball* and reward with the ball (and a treat if needed).

Teach the Meaning:

MEANING: *Ball* is a noun, referring to a specific small, object type. It is a type of *Toy.*

1. Entice (cue with *Sign Toy*). When she does, show the toy meaning by giving her the ball (then a treat if needed).
2. Put the toy ball in front of your dog.
3. When she looks at it, sign/say *IS Toy.*

4. Entice (cue with *Sign Ball*) your dog to sign *Ball.*

5. When she does, show the meaning by giving her the ball (then a treat if needed).

6. Put the ball in front of your dog.

7. When she looks at it, sign/say *IS Ball* (or *IS Toy Ball*).

Test the Student:

1. When your dog is looking at the ball, sign/say *What IS That?*

2. When she signs *Toy,* sign/say *Yes! Toy* and reward with the ball.

3. As your dog is looking at the ball, sign/say *What Type IS That?*

4. If your student doesn't sign *Ball,* don't say *Na,* just tell your dog to *Sign Ball.*

5. When she does, sign/say *Yes! Ball* and give her the ball.

Practice Exercises

Practice *Ball* in various locations. Perform these exercises in order. With your dog watching, place a ball on top of a pillow.

- Say/sign *What Type IS That?*
- When your dog signs *Ball,* sign/say *Yes! Ball* and give it to her.

With your dog watching, place a ball *under* the pillow.

- Say/sign *What Type IS That?* Point to the area under the pillow.
- When your dog signs *Ball,* sign/say *Yes! Ball* and give it to her.

Before and during playtime with a ball, do the following before you reward with a ball:

- As she looks at the ball, ask her *What IS That?*
- If your dog signs *Toy,* sign/say *Yes! Toy* and give it to her.
- Ask her *What Type IS That?*
- When your dog signs *Ball,* sign/say *Yes! Ball* and give her the ball for a while.

Tips

Be sure to have taught *Toy* before teaching any toy types, as in *Ball.* If, when you ask for *Ball,* your dog signs *Toy,* use guided feedback (*Yah* to *Yes!*) to shape the gesture. Do not say *Na* (or *No*). Adjust the leg position by slowly pushing the leg toward the left. Use *Freeze* to instruct her to hold the correct position. When she responds correctly, sign/say *Yes! Ball.*

Some dogs will want toy rewards, others want food rewards. When your dog doesn't consider the ball reward enough, give the ball and immediately follow with a treat. This is how Chal learned many of the toy types. She prefers food rewards.

If your dog is persistently confused about the difference between *Toy* and *Ball,* then skip the *What Type IS That?* for a while. During the break, work with the move for *Ball,* separate from the meaning. Learn other words in broad categories (*Food, Toy, Animal, Thing*), rather than types. Continue to pile up tricks (cued moves). The time will come when you'll need them quickly.

Comments

Your dog learning *Toy* and *Ball* is significant. She knows that movements from different legs result in different responses from you. She now also knows that different movements from the same limb also provoke different responses from you. These additional gestures increase the vocabulary your dog has to communicate with. She will take advantage of this soon.

SIGN: FRISBEE

GESTURE: As you sign, say the word *Frisbee.*

The *human* gesture starts in a sit or stand position, hand at the side. Move your straight right arm, up high in front of you, then down.

The *dog* gesture starts in a sit (or stand) position. Your dog should move her straight right front leg up high, then down. This is a specific movement.

Teach the Move:

1. Entice your dog to make the move.

   - If you model this gesture facing your dog, use your left arm to mirror what she should do, with her right front leg.

   - Catch your dog making the natural move.

   - Lure the leg into the correct position with the Frisbee.

- Mold, direct, and adjust the leg.
- Use other techniques listed in the model instructions, as needed.

2. When she moves correctly, sign/say *Yes! Frisbee* and give or throw the Frisbee.

CHAL SIGNING FRISBEE

Cue the Move:

1. Entice the move, then sign/say *Sign Frisbee.*
2. Repeat until you can sign/say *Sign Frisbee,* and your dog signs *Frisbee.*
3. Say/sign *Yes! Frisbee* and reward with the Frisbee.

Teach the Meaning:

MEANING: The word *Frisbee* is a noun, referring to a *specific* small, object type. If you don't use the Frisbee, replace this word with a toy your dog really likes to play with. It is a *Toy* word.

1. Entice (cue with *Sign Toy*) your dog to sign *Toy.* When she does, show the toy meaning by giving her the Frisbee (then a treat if needed).
2. Put the toy Frisbee in front of your dog. When she looks at it, sign/ say *IS Toy.*

3. Entice (cue with *Sign Toy*) your dog to sign *Toy.* When she does, show the meaning by giving her the Frisbee (and a treat if needed).

4. Put a Frisbee in front of your dog. When she looks at it, sign/say *IS Frisbee* (or *IS Toy Frisbee*).

Test the Student:

1. When your dog is looking at the Frisbee, sign/say *What IS That?*

2. When she signs *Toy,* sign/say *Yes! Toy* and reward with the Frisbee.

3. When your dog is looking at the Frisbee, sign/say *What Type IS That?*

4. If your student doesn't sign *Frisbee,* tell your dog to *Sign Frisbee.*

5. When she does, sign/say *Yes! Frisbee* and give her the Frisbee for a while.

Practice Exercises

Practice *Frisbee* in various locations. Perform these exercises in order. With your dog watching, place a Frisbee on *top* of a pillow.

- Say/sign *What Type IS That?*
- When your dog signs, sign/say *Yes! Frisbee* and give it to her.

With your dog watching, place a Frisbee *under* the pillow.

- Say/sign *What Type IS That?* Point to the area under the pillow.
- When your dog signs *Frisbee,* sign/say *Yes! Frisbee* and give it to her.

Before and during playtime with a Frisbee, do the following, before you reward with a Frisbee:

- Ask her *What IS That?*
- If your dog signs *Toy,* sign/say *Yes! Toy* and give it to her.
- Ask her *What Type IS That?*
- If your student doesn't sign *Frisbee,* cue her to *Sign Frisbee.*
- When your dog signs *Frisbee,* sign/say *Yes! Frisbee* and give her the Frisbee for a while.

Tips

Be sure to have taught *Toy* before working on *Frisbee* (or the sign for another favorite toy). This sign is for your dog's favorite toy (thus the high leg move). If your dog doesn't play with or like the Frisbee, use a different toy and word for this move (*Duck, Rope, Squeeky,* etc.)

If, when you ask for *Frisbee,* your dog signs *Toy,* use guided feedback (*Yah* to *Yes!*) to shape the gesture. Adjust the leg position by slowly pushing the leg toward the left. Use *Freeze* to instruct her to hold the correct position. When correct, sign/say feedback *Yes! Frisbee.* Do not say *No* or *Na.*

If your dog is persistently confused about the difference between *Toy* and *Frisbee,* then skip the *What Type IS That?* for a while. During that break, work with the move for *Frisbee,* separate from the meaning. Learn other words in broad categories rather than types. Continue to pile up tricks (cued moves). The time will come when you'll need them quickly.

Comments

Your dog learning *Toy* and *Frisbee* is significant. She knows that movements from different legs result in different responses from you. She now also knows that different movements from the same limb provoke other responses from you. Using these different gestures increases her vocabulary and opportunity to communicate with you.

Toy words are useful for developing communication and language in dogs. As your dog has different favorite toys, name them using the *Name* sign techniques in the Gestuary. If your dog already has a unique move, cue the move to make it easy to teach her a new meaning for it—a new word.

SIGN: DOOR

GESTURE: As you sign, say the word *Door.*

The *human* gesture starts in a standing position, hands at your side. Move your bent right forearm up in front of your body to waist level, with limp wrist, palm down.

The *dog* gesture starts in a standing position. Your dog should move her bent right front leg up, paw down. This is a specific movement.

Teach the Move:

1. Entice your dog to make the move.

- If you model this gesture facing your dog, use your left arm to mirror what she should do with her right front leg.
- Catch your dog making the natural move.
- Mold, direct, and adjust the leg from the upper leg region.
- Use other techniques listed in the model instructions, as needed.

CHAL SIGNING DOOR

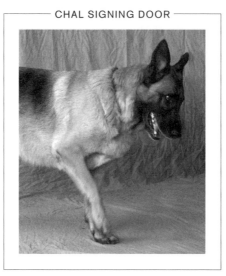

2. When she moves correctly, sign/say *Yes! Door* and reward with a treat.

Cue the Move:

1. Entice the move, then sign/say *Sign Door.*
2. Repeat until you can sign/say *Sign Door* and your dog signs *Door.*
3. Say/sign *Yes! Door,* touch or open the door, and give a treat.

Teach the Meaning:

MEANING: *Door* is a noun, referring to a specific object type.

1. Entice (cue with *Sign Door*) your dog to sign *Door.* When she does, show the meaning by tapping the door.
2. Stand your dog in front of a door, and place your hand on the door. When she looks at it, sign/say *IS Door.*

Test the Student:

1. Stand your dog in front of a door.

2. When she is looking at it, sign/say **What's That?**

3. When she signs **Toy,** sign/say **Yes! Toy** and tap the door and treat her.

4. When your dog is looking at the door, sign/say **What Type IS That?**

5. When she signs **Door,** sign/say **Yes! Door,** open it, go out, and then treat her.

Practice Exercises

Practice **Door** in front of various doors—front, bedroom, patio, crate, dog, etc. Help your dog generalize the concept. With your dog watching, tap the door.

- Say/sign **IS Door.**

- Say/sign **Sign Door.** When she does, tap the door, and reward.

- Say/sign **What Type IS That?**

- When your dog signs **Door,** sign/say **Yes! Door** and reward.

To start learning **Open Door,** distinct from identifying a **Door,** place your dog by the front door.

- Say/sign **IS Door.**

- Say/sign **Sign Door.** When she does, touch the door, and reward.

- Say/sign **What Type IS That?**

- When your dog signs **Door,** sign/say **Yes! Door** and reward.

- Say/sign **Sign Door.**

- When she does, swing her right bent leg to the right (like a swing door) as you say **Door Open.**

- Open the door wide and go out.

- Try this several times from inside and outside.

- At the door, ask her **What?** (Don't say **That** or point.)

- Entice her (in various ways) to sign **Door Open.**

- When she signs **Door Open,** open the door and go out.

Tips

Be sure to have taught *Toy* before attempting *Door,* and *Door* before attempting *Door Open.*

If you ask for *Door* but your dog signs *Toy,* use guided feedback (*Yah* to *Yes!*) to shape the gesture. Manually adjust the leg position. Then use *Freeze* to instruct her to hold the correct position. When correct, sign/say feedback *Yes! Door.*

If your dog does this, tap your dog's right paw with your toes (lightly). Your dog will lift her right leg, then tap the door, saying *IS Door.* Don't open it, yet. Say *Door Open,* before you do.

Comments

The *Door* gesture is different than the other signs we've been learning. It can be a large or small object, and can open and close. Though alone this sign is not a verb, your dog may use it to mean *Open The Door.* Take the liberty to use it as a noun or verb. Or use it as a noun but teach your dog to sway the *Door* sign to mean *Open The Door.*

Learning *Door* is usually easy for dogs. They will often go to a door and wait for you to open it. If you stand there and just look at them, some will lift their leg to get you to do something.

Try extending the sign to all doors in your house. Teach your dog to label specific doors: using the sign explained above for the main door, performing the sign twice for your bedroom, three times for the kid's room, etc. Or you can teach your dog to sign *Door* followed by someone's name to denote that person's door. For your bedroom, use *Door Name1;* for her room (or crate) use *Door Name0.* (See *Name* signs on page 178.)

Chal signed *Door* easily, while we were waiting by the front door. Having her practice the sign in front of her crate and dog doors helped her generalize.

SIGN: BED

GESTURE: As you sign, say the word *Bed.*

The *human* gesture starts in a standing position, hands at your side. Move your straight right arm forward and down, with palm facing the ground. People make this move when indicating by patting an area for a dog to come lay down.

The *dog* gesture starts in a standing position. Your dog should move her straight right front leg up and reach forward. This is a specific movement looking much like reaching out to grab the bed.

CHAL SIGNING BED

Teach the Move:

1. Entice your dog to make the move.

   - If you model this gesture facing your dog, use your left arm to mirror what she should do with her right front leg.

   - Catch your dog making the natural move.

   - Mold, direct, and adjust the leg, keeping it straight.

   - Use other techniques listed in the model instructions, as needed.

2. When she moves correctly, sign/say *Yes! Bed* and reward with a treat.

Cue the Move:

1. Entice the move, then sign/say *Sign Bed.*

2. Repeat until you can sign/say *Sign Bed* and your dog signs *Bed.*

3. Say/sign *Yes! Bed,* pat the bed, and give a treat.

Teach the Meaning:

MEANING: ***Bed*** is a noun, referring to a *specific* object type.

1. Entice (cue with ***Sign Bed***) your dog to sign ***Bed***.

2. When she does, show the meaning by patting the bed.

3. Stand your dog in front of her bed.

4. When she looks at it, sign/say ***IS Bed***.

Test the Student:

1. Stand your dog in front of her bed.

2. When she is looking at it, sign/say ***What's That?***

3. When she signs ***Toy***, sign/say ***Yes! Toy*** and tap the door and treat her.

4. When your dog is looking at the bed, sign/say ***What Type IS That?***

5. When she signs ***Bed***, sign/say ***Yes! Bed*** and pat the bed.

Practice Exercises

Practice ***Bed*** in front of various beds, especially in areas where she lies down, such as the couch, your bed, her bed. This will help your dog generalize the concept. With your dog watching, pat (with your foot or hand) the bed.

• Say/sign ***IS Bed***.

• Say/sign ***Sign Bed***. When she does, pat the bed, and reward.

• Say/sign ***What Type IS That?***

• When your dog signs ***Bed***, sign/say ***Yes! Bed*** and reward.

To associate function of the bed, have your dog go to the bed then ask her to identify it. Place your dog a few feet from her bed.

• Say ***Go To*** then sign ***Bed***.

• If she doesn't walk to the bed, guide her.

• When she arrives, say ***Yes! Bed***.

• Sign/say ***What Type IS That?***

• When your dog signs ***Bed***, sign/say ***Yes! Bed*** and reward.

In order to help your dog generalize that the bed is a bed anywhere, do the following:

- With your dog watching, move her bed to a different spot in the room, or bring in a different small "bed."
- Ask her, sign/say **What Type IS That?**
- If she doesn't respond, entice or cue her to sign **Bed.**
- When your dog signs **Bed,** sign/say **Yes! Bed** and reward

Tips

Be sure to have taught **Toy** before attempting **Bed,** and **Bed** before attempting **Go To Bed.**

If you ask for **Bed,** but your dog signs **Toy,** use guided feedback (**Yah** to **Yes!**) to shape the gesture. Manually adjust the leg position to be straight out and forward. Use **Freeze** to instruct her to hold the correct position. When correct, sign/say feedback **Yes! Bed.**

If your dog doesn't reach out with her right front leg straight, lure the leg with a treat she needs to reach for.

Comments

Teach **Bed** after mastering **Toy.** Learning **Bed** is usually easy for dogs as they cherish the space. Try extending the sign to all beds in your house. An advanced exercise is to teach your dog to name or label specific beds by combining **Name** signs with the **Bed** sign, as in your bed (**Bed Name1**) or your dog's bed (**Bed Name0**). The bed word comes before the identifier name.

Chal signed **Bed** easily when I brought home a new bed for her. We played with the bed; she layed down on it. Taking advantage of her intense interest in the bed, I taught her the gesture for it right then.

SIGN: PHONE

GESTURE: As you sign, say the word **Phone.**

The *human* gesture starts in a sit or stand position, right hand at your right ear, palm facing your ear (as in holding a phone). Move your hand from your ear brushing down past your mouth.

The *dog* gesture starts in a standing position. Your dog should move her right front leg from her ear down toward her jaw. This is a specific movement.

Teach the Move:

1. Entice your dog to make the move.

   • If you model this gesture facing your dog, use your left arm to mirror what she should do with her right front leg.

   • Catch your dog making the natural move when rubbing her face.

   • Mold, direct, and adjust the leg to make the move.

   • Use other techniques listed in the model instructions, as needed.

—— CHAL SIGNING PHONE ——

2. When she moves correctly, sign/say **Yes! Phone** and reward with a treat.

Cue the Move:

1. Entice the move, then sign/say **Sign Phone.**

2. Repeat until you can sign/say **Sign Phone** and your dog signs **Phone.**

3. Say/sign **Yes! Phone,** handle a phone, and give a treat.

Teach the Meaning:

MEANING: The word **Phone** is a noun, referring to a specific object type. You may teach it as a general or specific word.

1. Entice (cue with **Sign Phone**) your dog to sign **Phone.**

2. When she does, show the meaning by showing her the phone, then reward with a treat.

3. Stand your dog in front of a phone.

4. When she looks at it, sign/say *IS Phone.*

Test the Student:

1. Stand your dog in front of a phone.

2. When she is looking at it, sign/say *What's That?*

3. When she signs *Toy,* sign/say *Yes! Toy* and tap the phone, and treat her.

4. When your dog is looking at the phone, sign/say *What Type IS That?*

5. When she signs *Phone,* sign/say *Yes! Phone*, show her the phone, and reward.

Practice Exercises

Practice *Phone* in various places with different phones. Help your dog generalize the concept by using the phones in front of her. With your dog watching, have someone call you. Speak into the phone. Have someone talk back.

- Say/sign *IS Phone.*
- Say/sign *Sign Phone.* When she does, tap the phone and reward.
- Say/sign *What Type IS That?*
- When your dog signs *Phone,* sign/say *Yes! Phone* and reward.

To reinforce the meaning of *Phone* (it rings and people's voices come out of it), place your dog by the phone and answering machine. To challenge your dog, we are going to push word learning. Have someone available to call you so the phone rings and the person can leave a message. If you can, get another person (Person2) to place the call and talk on the phone. Practice each group of instructions as different lessons. Don't do them all on the same call.

- Have Person2 dial from elsewhere. When the phone rings, sign/say *IS Phone.*
- Say/sign *Sign Phone.* When your dog signs, touch the phone to her and reward.

- Have Person2 repeat the call. This time when it rings, sign/say *What IS That?*
- If your dog doesn't sign, sign/say *Sign Phone.*
- When your dog signs, touch the phone to her and reward.

Tips

Teach *Toy* before attempting *Phone.* If your dog has trouble making the *move* correctly, have some thick transparent or masking tape, and be ready for quick action.

- Place a piece of tape on the back (or front for large dogs) of the right ear.
- As your dog tries to take the tape off with her right paw, sign/say *Yes! Phone* and reward. Don't let her swallow the tape.
- Using the clicker after you say *Yes!* above makes this easy.
- Repeat these steps above several times.
- Go back to and repeat the sections on Cue the Move, Teach the Meaning, and finally, Test the Student.

If, when you ask for *Phone,* your dog signs *Toy,* be sure you are asking *What Type IS That?*, not *What's That?* Use guided feedback (*Yah* to *Yes!*) to shape the gesture. Manually adjust the leg position. When your dog moves correctly, sign/say feedback *Yes! Phone.*

Signing *Phone* is harder for larger or older dogs. It takes more energy to lift a large leg up toward the ear. Accept a smaller gesture for the larger or older dog, allowing the paw to move down from the eye region to the mouth.

Comments

Learning *Phone* is easy for dogs to understand. They will often go to a ringing phone and wait for you to make it stop ringing. (Chal gets a treat for that.)

You may teach your dog to tell you if your phone is vibrating (if you forgot to turn it back on) rather than ringing. Teach her to sign *Phone* when it vibrates (a cue for phone).

Alerting dogs can tell you the phone is ringing without bringing you to the phone, as you may or not want to answer. You might be able to teach your dog to tell you who is leaving a message on the phone.

Chal made the **Phone** move on her own. She generalized **Phone** quickly to all phones. She tends to bark at me if I stay on any phone too long.

Chal knows a friend of mine, Debbie. Chal recognized Debbie's voice in person and on the phone. One day Debbie left a loud voice message. While I listened to it, I asked Chal, **Who's That?** Chal turned her head to the left, which she had learned was the gesture for Debbie's name. The phone, the answering machine, and I were all on Chal's right, not left, side. This suggests she was not cued to sign **Debbie.**

You may want to extend the sign, and teach your dog to label specific Phones—perhaps by the sign above for the main **Phone,** tapping the floor once for your bedroom, twice for the kid's room, etc. Or, you can teach her to sign **Phone** followed by someone's name. If it is your bedroom, use **Phone Name1,** for her room use **Phone Name0,** whether a crate or a real room.

SIGN: CAR

GESTURE: As you sign, say the word **Car.**

The *human* gesture starts in stand position. Move your right knee slightly up, forward, then down. Your foot should land in front of its start position.

The *dog* gesture starts in a stand position. Your dog should move her right hind leg slightly up, forward, then down. Her leg should land in front of its start position.

Teach the Move:

1. Entice your dog to make the move.
   - If you model this gesture facing your dog, use the left leg to mirror what she should do with her right hind leg.
   - Model the move yourself for your dog to imitate.
   - Catch your dog making the natural move.
   - Tap, from behind, your dog's hind leg.
   - Use other techniques listed in the model instructions, as needed.
2. When she does this, sign/say **Yes! Car** and reward.

CHAL SIGNING CAR

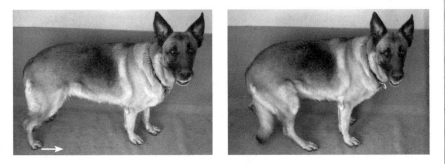

Cue the Move:

1. Entice the move, then sign/say ***Sign Car.***

2. Repeat until you can sign/say ***Sign Car*** and your dog then signs ***Car.***

3. Sign/say ***Yes! Car*** and reward.

Teach the Meaning:

MEANING: ***Car*** is a noun, a specific object label, that refers to a large motor vehicle, that your dog cannot handle as a toy.

1. Entice (cue with ***Sign Car***) your dog to sign ***Car.***

2. When she does, show the meaning by having her interact with the outside of the car.

3. When your dog is attending to the car, sign/say ***IS Car.***

Test the Student:

1. When your dog is attending to the car, sign/say ***What's That?***

2. When she signs ***Thing,*** sign/say ***Yes! Thing,*** tap the car, and treat her.

3. When your dog is looking at the car, sign/say ***What Type IS That?***

4. If your student doesn't sign ***Car,*** entice (cue with ***Sign Car***).

5. When she signs correctly, sign/say ***Yes! Car,*** tap it, and reward her with a treat.

Practice Exercises

Practice **Car** with one car, in one place at first, then in various locations. Later practice with different cars, then in different places. Perform these exercises in order. Encourage your dog to interact (sniff, touch) the car.

- Say/sign **IS Car,** as you touch the car.
- Ask your dog to **Sign Car.** When she does, reward with a treat.
- Ask your dog **What's That?**
- When your dog signs **Car,** sign/say **Yes! Car** and reward.

Interact (you and dog) with the car parked in a different spot. Follow the same steps as above. Next, interact (you and dog) with the car from a different angle, side, front, and rear doors. Follow the same steps as above. Finally, interact with a group of cars in a parking lot.

- Walk past each car, enticing your dog to notice each thing.
- Say/sign **IS Car,** as you touch the car.
- Go back again past each car, enticing your dog to notice each thing.
- Stop at each car and ask your dog to **Sign Car.** When she does, reward with a treat.
- Go back yet again, past each car, enticing your dog to notice each thing.
- Stop at each car and ask your dog **What's That?**
- When your dog signs **Thing,** sign/say **Yes! Thing** and reward.
- Go back yet again, past each car, enticing your dog to notice each thing.
- Stop at each car and ask your dog **What Type IS That?**
- When your dog signs **Car,** sign/say **Yes! Car** and reward.

Tips

Attempt this sign after your dog knows and uses the **Thing** gesture. Most dogs don't make this exact move often, so you'll need to guide your dog to move her back leg a bit forward.

If you must use a food reward for a **Car** sign, be sure to touch the car first, then give the treat. If you give the treat first, your dog won't pay attention to the car.

Don't say anything if your dog moves incorrectly; just wait, encourage, and help her along with guided practice and feedback. Practice even if you are not seeing an obvious result. Some dogs take a bit longer to process. Eventually they will learn it well.

If your dog is not associating the meaning of **Car** with the move, just continue to familiarize your dog with all the car parts.

Before you go for a ride, in front of the car, ask your dog to **Sign Car.**

Hide a treat in the car, ask your dog to **Sign Car** and when she does, open the car door and let your dog find the treat.

Comments

The **Car** gesture is a bit more difficult to teach than **Thing.** But there are many opportunities to teach it. The move is more challenging due to the forward movement of the back leg. The meaning is more challenging than **Toy,** since the object is large and not as easily focused on in one glance. A dog in front of a car might notice the car door rather than the whole car. By testing the sign at various car spots, your dog will understand that **Car** means any part of the car or the whole car. By your demonstrating the significance (to your dog) of cars, she will be motivated to learn the sign. Convey significance by taking your dog for a ride after she signs **Car.**

SIGN: HUMAN

GESTURE: As you sign, say the word **Human.**

The *human* gesture starts in stand position. Move your left knee up and forward, then back down. Your foot should land in front of its start position.

The *dog* gesture starts in a stand position. Your dog should move her left hind foot up and forward. Her foot should land in front of its start position then back down.

Teach the Move:

1. Entice your dog to make the move.
   - Model the move yourself for your dog to imitate. If you model this gesture facing your dog, use the right leg to mirror what she should do with her left hind leg.
   - Catch your dog making the natural move.

- Tap your dog's hind leg.
- Use other techniques listed in the model instructions, as needed.

CHAL SIGNING HUMAN

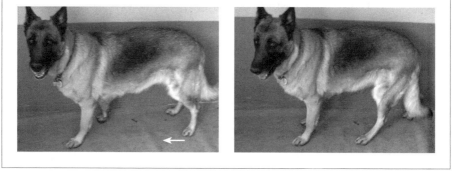

2. When she does this, sign/say **Yes! Human** and reward.

Cue the Move:

1. Entice the move, then sign/say **Sign Human.**
2. Repeat until you can sign/say **Sign Human** and your dog then signs **Human.**
3. Sign/say **Yes! Human** and reward.

MEANING: **Human** is a noun, a specific object label, that refers to a person.

Teach the Meaning:

1. Entice (cue with **Sign Human**) your dog to sign **Human.**
2. When she does, show the meaning by having her interact (safely) with a person.
3. When your dog is attending to the person, sign/say **IS Human.**

Test the Student:

1. When your dog is attending to the person, sign/say **What's That?**
2. If your student doesn't sign **Animal,** entice (cue with **Sign Animal**).
3. When she signs correctly, sign/say **Yes! Animal** and reward with a treat (or appropriate play with that person).

4. When your dog is attending to the person, sign/say *What Type IS That?*

5. If your student doesn't sign *Human,* entice (cue with *Sign Human*).

6. When she signs correctly, sign/say *Yes! Human* and reward with a treat (or appropriate play with that person).

Practice Exercises

Practice *Human* with one person at first, then in various locations. Later practice with different people, then in different places. Perform these exercises in order with a human friend.

- Say/sign *IS Human,* as you touch the person.
- Ask your dog to *Sign Human.* When she does, reward (with treat or with fun interaction with that person).
- Ask your dog *What Type IS That?*
- When your dog signs *Human,* sign/say *Yes! Human* and reward.

Next, interact with the person in a different place. Follow the same steps as above. Finally, interact with a group of people at a calm gathering.

- Walk past each person, enticing your dog to notice each one.
- Say/sign *IS Human,* as you touch or point to each.
- Go back again past each person, enticing your dog to notice each one.
- Stop by each person and ask your dog to *Sign Human.* When she does, reward with interaction and a treat.
- Go back yet again, past each person, enticing your dog to notice each one.
- Stop at each person and ask your dog *What's That?*
- When your dog signs *Animal,* sign/say *Yes! Animal* and reward with fun interaction and a treat.
- When your dog is attending to the person, sign/say *What Type IS That?*
- If your student doesn't sign *Human,* entice (cue with *Sign Human*).

- When she signs correctly, sign/say **Yes! Human** and reward with a treat (or appropriate play with that person).

Tips

Teach **Human** after mastering **Animal.** Most dogs make this move when walking. You can wait for your dog to make the move herself, then sign/say **Yes! Human** and reward.

If your dog doesn't make this move easily, you can lightly tap your foot on your dog's paw; she should lift her foot straight up, down, and forward. Then you sign/say **Sign Human** and reward.

If you must use a food reward instead of an interaction for the **Human** sign, be sure to show, touch, point to the person before giving the treat. You or the person may give the treat. If you give the treat first, your dog won't pay attention the person.

If your dog is not associating the meaning of **Human** with the move, just continue to familiarize your dog with **Human** by saying **IS Human** often. Use it when someone is at the door, when your dog is interested in a guest, or when you come home. You, being a human, can point to yourself while saying **IS Human** or **What's Type IS That?**

Comments

The **Human** gesture is relatively easy to teach as there are many opportunities to do so.

Search and rescue (SAR) dogs might be interested in these terms (in addition to **Dead** and **Alive**) to potentially specifically identify the found animal type (human, dog, cat, deer, cat, bird, etc.) and condition (living or dead). After an earthquake, a signing SAR dog could search under rubble and might be able communicate details of her discovery, signing **Four Humans, Two Dead, Two Alive.**

ADVANCED SIGNS:
5 Names

Teach the Advanced signs after you and your canine students have mastered the Basic/Foundation and some of the Intermediate signs.

SIGN: NAME (NAME1, NAME2, NAME3, NAME4, NAME0)

The *Name* signs are made with head moves and refer to important people or animals (in your dog's life). *Name1* is your dog's most significant other, you. (*Name1* for my dog is me, *Sean.*) *Name2* is whomever is next in line, *Name3* is a close friend, *Name0* is the dog herself, and *Name4* is a stranger, unnamed friend, or unwelcome person.

Name0 for my dog is *Chal.*

SIGN: NAME1–YOU

GESTURE: As you sign, say the word *Name1.* Since my name is Sean, I would say *Sean* rather than *Name1.* You would say your name instead.

The *human* move starts with you next to your dog facing the same direction, hands at your side. Move your head to your right, then quickly back to center. (When you teach this, facing your dog, you'll move your head to the left.) Keep your eyes focused downward so as not to suggest your dog go to the direction you are moving your head.

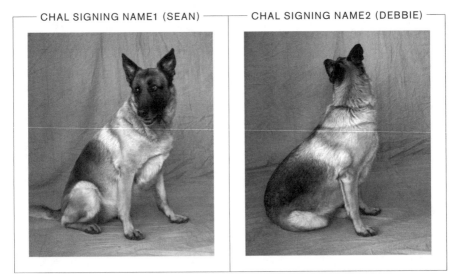

|— CHAL SIGNING NAME1 (SEAN) —|— CHAL SIGNING NAME2 (DEBBIE) —|

The *dog* move starts with her head facing forward. The dog should move only her head and/or neck to her right (slightly up), then quickly back to center. Dogs make this move when they look at you as you lead them at your side.

NAME1

Teach the Move:

1. Entice your dog to make the move.

   - Catch your dog making the natural head move to her right.

   - Move your hand (with treat) to lure your dog's head to her right.

   - Move your hand (without the treat) to lure your dog's head to her right.

2. Say/sign *Yes!* and reward from center.

Cue the Move:

1. Entice the move and sign/say *Sign Name1.*

2. When successful, sign/say *Sign Name1.*

3. Repeat until you can just sign/say *Sign Name1* and your dog signs *Name1,* then reward.

Teach the Meaning:

MEANING: The word *Name1* is name of the dog's most significant person—you.

1. Have an assistant in front of your dog, and you stand at your dog's right.

2. Have the assistant point to you and sign/say *IS Name1.* (Don't let your dog go to you.)

3. Have your assistant cue the move by signing/saying *Sign Name1.*

4. Your dog should sign *Name1* (looking at you).

5. Sign/say *Yes! Name1* and reward.

6. Hide behind an object (to your dog's right).

7. Have your assistant cue the move by signing/saying *Sign Name1* while you step out from the right.

8. Hide behind an object (to your dog's right) and then appear.

9. Have your assistant cue the move, by signing/saying *Sign Name1.*

10. Your dog should sign *Name1* (looking at you).

11. Say/sign *Yes! Name1* and reward. (Usually a playful scratch or hug will do.)

Test the Student:

Test your dog's skill at names by doing the following:

1. With you in various positions around your dog, have an assistant say/sign *Who's That?,* referring to you.

2. When your dog signs *Name1,* sign/say *Yes! Name1* and reward.

Practice Exercises

Practice *Name1* in various locations, inside and outside, in front of and behind doors or curtains. Perform these exercises in order: stand in front of your door, to your dog's right.

- Have an assistant sign/say *Who's That?,* referring to you.
- When your dog signs *Name1,* sign/say *Yes! Name1* and reward.

Stand in the open doorway, facing your dog.

- Have an assistant sign/say *Who's That?,* referring to you.
- When your dog signs *Name1,* sign/say *Yes! Name1* and reward.

Stand on the other side of the closed doorway, then knock.

- Have an assistant sign/say *Who's That?,* referring to you (not visible).
- When your dog signs *Name1,* sign/say *Yes! Name1* and open the door and reward profusely.

If your dog is not signing your name but rather pointing to your location, try the following exercises:

- Have an assistant in front of, and you stand at, your dog's right.
- Have the assistant casually point to you and sign/say *IS Name1.* (This is not a *Go To* request, so don't let your dog go to you.)
- Hide behind an object (at your dog's right).
- Have your assistant sign/say *Sign Name1,* as you step out from the right.

- Your dog should sign *Name1.*
- Say/sign *Yes! Name1.*
- Repeat the steps oppposite, but next practice standing in front of your dog's right of center, then practice with you at her front center, then left of center, then left. Your dog should always sign to her right (not to where you are).

Tips

If you or your assistant find it too complicated to both say and sign the these K9Signs, just say the words.

If your dog doesn't sign *Name1* at the door or if she can't see you, have the assistant cue her by signing/saying *Sign Name1.* Or have the assistant lure your dog with a treat to her right.

If your dog still looks at you wherever you are, use a treat to lure your dog to the correct head position.

SIGN: NAME2

GESTURE: As you sign, say the word *Name2.* Since my friend's name is Debbie, I would say Debbie rather than *Name2.* You would say your friend's name instead.

The *human* move starts with you by your dog's side both facing forward, hands to your side. Move your head to your left side, then quickly back to center. (If you teach facing your dog, you'll need to move your head to your right.) Keep your eyes focused downward so as not to suggest your dog go anywhere.

The *dog* move starts with her head facing forward. The dog should move only her head and/or neck to her left (slightly up), then quickly back to center. Dogs make this move when they look at someone standing at their left.

Teach the Move:

1. Entice your dog to make the move.
   - Catch your dog making the natural head move to her left.
   - Move your hand (with treat) to lure your dog's head to her left.
   - Move your hand (without the treat) to lure you dog's head to her left.
2. Say/sign *Yes! Name2* and reward from center.

Cue the Move:

1. Entice the move, and sign/say ***Sign Name2.***

2. When successful, sign/say ***Sign Name2*** and reward.

3. Repeat steps on the previous page until you can just sign/say ***Sign Name2*** and your dog signs ***Name2,*** then reward.

Teach the Meaning:

MEANING: ***Name2*** is name of the dog's next-in-line significant person—Person2.

1. Stand in front, and Person2 stand at the left, of your dog.

2. Point to Person2 and sign/say ***IS Name2.*** (Don't let your dog go to Person2.)

3. Cue the move by signing/saying ***Sign Name2.***

4. Your dog should sign ***Name2*** (looking at Person2).

5. Say/sign ***Yes! Name2*** and reward.

6. Have Person2 hide behind an object (to your dog's left).

7. Cue the move by signing/saying ***Sign Name2.***

8. Person2 steps out from the left.

9. Have Person2 hide, then step out to be seen.

10. Cue your dog with ***Sign Name2.***

11. When she does, sign/say ***Yes! Name2*** and reward.

Test the Student:

With Person2 in various positions around your dog, do the following:

1. Say/sign ***Who's That?,*** referring to Person2.

2. When your dog signs ***Name2,*** sign/say ***Yes! Name2*** and reward.

3. Move Person2 to a new spot and repeat steps above.

Practice Exercises

Practice ***Name2*** in various locations, inside and outside, in front of and behind doors or curtains.

Have Person2 stand in front of your door, to your dog's left, and perform these in order.

- Say/sign ***Who's That?,*** referring to Person2.

- When your dog signs *Name2,* sign/say *Yes! Name2* and reward.

Have Person2 should stand in the open doorway, facing your dog.
- Say/sign *Who's That?* referring to Person2.
- When your dog signs *Name2,* sign/say *Yes! Name2* and reward.

Have Person2 stand on the other side of the closed doorway, then knock.
- Say/sign *Who's That?,* referring to Person2 (not visible).
- When your dog signs *Name2,* sign/say *Yes! Name2* and open the door and reward profusely.

If your dog is not signing Person2's name but rather pointing to her location, try the following exercises:
- Stand in front of your dog. Person2 stands at your dog's left.
- Casually point to Person2 and sign/say *IS Name2.* (This is not a *Go To* request, so don't let your dog move.)
- Have Person2 hide behind an object (at your dog's left).
- Say/sign *Sign Name2* as Person2 steps out from the left.
- Your dog should sign *Name2.* Sign/say *Yes! Name2* and reward.

Repeat the exercises above, with Person2 standing in front of you dog's left of center, then at center, right of center, then right. Your dog should always sign to her left (not to where Person2 is).

If your dog has learned to sign *Phone,* challenge her with this exercise combining *Phone* and *Name2.* You will be asking your dog to identify the phone and the voice of Person2, whom the dog knows how to name (*Name2*).
- With your dog attentive to the phone, have the Person2 call and talk loudly on the phone, saying your dog's name (*Hi Name0*) several times slowly.
- You sign/say *IS Name2,* in *Phone.*
- Sign/say *Who's That?*
- If your dog doesn't sign *Name2* cue with *Sign Name2.*
- When your dog signs *Name2,* reward profusely with several treats and have Person2 sign/say *Yes! Name2, Good Girl.*
- From the phone, have Person2 say *Good-Bye, Name0.*
- Sign/say *What's That?* Or *What Type IS That?*

- When your dog signs *Toy,* or *Phone* (respectively), reward.
- Then hang up and praise your dog.

Tips

If you, your friend, or your assistant find it too complicated to both say and sign the K9Signs, just say the words.

If your dog doesn't sign *Name2* at the door or if she can't see this person, cue her by signing/saying *Sign Name2.* Or lure your dog with a treat to her left.

If your dog still looks at you rather than names Person2, use a treat to lure your dog to the correct head position.

SIGN: NAME3

GESTURE: As you sign, say the word *Name3.* This is the name of yet another person or animal in your dog's life.

The *human* move starts with you facing your dog, hands at your side. Slowly tilt your head far up, then back down. Keep your eyes on your dog or straight ahead. This move differs from the head jerk up, as though you are pointing up with your head.

The *dog* move starts with her head facing forward. The dog should move her head and/or neck far up, then back down.

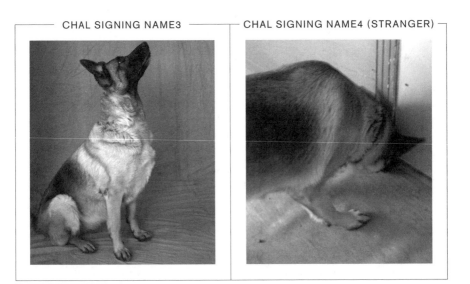

CHAL SIGNING NAME3 ——— CHAL SIGNING NAME4 (STRANGER)

Teach the Move:

1. Entice your dog to make the move.

   - Catch your dog making the head move up, then back down.

   - Move your hand (with treat) to lure your dog's head up, and move it back down.

   - Move your hand (without the treat) to lure your dog's head up, and move it back down.

2. Then sign/say *Yes!* and reward.

Cue the Move:

1. Entice the move, and sign/say *Sign Name3.*

2. When successful, sign/say *Sign Name3* and reward.

3. Repeat until you can just sign/say *Sign Name3* and your dog signs *Name3,* then reward.

Teach the Meaning:

MEANING: The word *Name3* is name of your dog's friend—Person3 (this can be an animal).

1. Stand in front of your dog. Person3 straddles your dog, so your dog has to look up to see Person3. Make sure your dog is comfortable with this. (If *Name3* is for a dog, you can skip this step.)

2. With treat in hand, point to Person3 and sign/say *IS Name3.*

3. Cue the move by signing/saying *Sign Name3.* With a treat, lure your dog to look up.

4. Say/sign *Yes! Name3* and reward.

5. Have Person3 hide, then step out to be seen.

6. Cue your dog with *Sign Name3.*

7. When she does, sign/say *Yes! Name3* and reward.

Test the Student:

Test your dog's skill at names by doing the following:

1. With Person3 in various positions around your dog, sign/say *Who's That?,* referring to Person3.

2. When your dog signs *Name3,* sign/say *Yes! Name3* and reward.

3. Move Person3 to a new spot and repeat.

Practice Exercises

Practice *Name3* in various locations, inside and outside, in front of and behind doors or curtains. Perform these in order.

Have Person3 straddle your dog (if your dog is comfortable with this).

- Say/sign *Who's That?,* referring to Person3.

- When your dog signs *Name3*, sign/say *Yes! Name3* and reward.

Have Person3 stand in the open doorway, facing your dog.

- Say/sign *Who's That?,* referring to Person3.

- When your dog signs *Name3*, sign/say *Yes! Name3* and reward.

Have Person3 stand on the other side of the closed doorway, then knock.

- Say/sign *Who's That?,* referring to Person3 (not visible).

- When your dog signs *Name3,* sign/say *Yes! Name3* and open the door and reward profusely.

If your dog is not signing Person3's name, have Person3 hold the treat, so your dog has to lift her head up to get it. (If Person3 is a dog, have an assistant hold the treat.)

Tips

If you, your friend, or your assistant find it too complicated to both say and sign the K9Signs, just say the word.

If your dog doesn't sign *Name3* at the door, or if she can't see this person, cue her by signing/saying *Sign Name3.* Or lure your dog into making the sign with a treat by moving it over her head.

If your dog still looks at you rather than names Person3, use a treat to lure your dog to the correct head position.

SIGN: NAME4–STRANGER

GESTURE: As you sign, say the word **Name4** (**Stranger**).

The *human* move starts with you facing your dog. Bending at your waist, move your head forward and down toward the ground. Your head should be as low as your waist.

The *dog* move starts with her head facing forward. The dog should move her head and/or neck forward and down toward the ground. Dogs make this move when looking at something apprehensively, and a similar move when searching for something on the ground.

Teach the Move:

1. Entice your dog to make the move.

   - Catch your dog making the head move down.

   - Move your hand (with treat), to lure your dog's head down to the ground.

2. Then sign/say **Yes! Name4** and reward.

Cue the Move:

1. Entice the move, and sign/say **Sign Name4.**

2. Fade any hand-treat cue, as your replace it with your signing/saying **Sign Name4** cue.

3. Entice the move with just your hand going to the floor, in front of her.

4. When successful, sign/say **Sign Name4** and reward.

5. Repeat until you can just sign/say **Sign Name4** and your dog signs **Name4**, then reward.

Teach the Meaning:

MEANING: The word **Name4** is another name. This can be a named friend, unnamed person, a stranger, or unwelcome person or animal. A stranger would be someone your dog has not yet, or briefly met, or a person whom your dog doesn't like. Instructions below are for a stranger who is unfamiliar. You may use this sign for any person or animal your dog knows. In that case, use the move here, the head down position, but follow instructions from this and the Name3.

1. Knowingly have a stranger (to your dog) knock at your door. With dog under control, as your dog barks, sign/say *IS Stranger.*

2. Cue the move by signing/saying *Sign Stranger.*

3. When she does, sign/say *Yes! Stranger* and reward.

4. Repeat the above steps with the same Stranger1, during the same encounter.

5. Repeat the above steps with a second Stranger2 (same session).

6. After your dog knows these people, they won't be strangers anymore. You'll have to find others.

Test the Student:

Test your dog's skill at names by doing the following.

1. With the Stranger1 in various safe positions around your dog, sign/say *Who's That?*, referring to the Stranger1.

2. When your dog signs *Stranger,* sign/say *Yes! Stranger* and reward.

3. With the Stranger2 in various safe positions around your dog, sign/say *Who's That?*, referring to the *Stranger2.*

4. When your dog signs *Stranger,* sign/say *Yes! Stranger* and reward.

Practice Exercises

Practice placing the Stranger in various locations—inside as well as outside, in front of and behind doors or curtains. Perform these exercises in one day, in order. The Stranger (who just entered your house for the above test) should step into the doorway to leave your home.

- Say/sign *Who's That?* referring to the Stranger.
- When your dog signs *Stranger,* sign/say *Yes! Stranger* and reward.

The Stranger should walk away from the house.

- Say/sign *Who's That?* referring to the Stranger.
- When your dog signs *Stranger,* sign/say *Yes! Stranger* and reward profusely.

Tips

If you, your friend, or your assistant find it too complicated to both say and sign the K9Signs, just say the words.

If your dog doesn't sign *Stranger* at the door, cue her by signing/saying *Sign Stranger.* Or lure your dog with a treat moved toward the floor.

Comments

Dogs do have a distinct bark and demeanor for strangers, for unwelcome or suspicious visitors, human or animal. Many people study and recognize those gestures and vocalizations. You can use these markers to help teach your dog a deliberate sign for one of those visitor types. You'll know the meaning and so will the dog.

Why teach this if your dog already knows a way to communicate something close to *Stranger?* To promote language development and mental stimulation. Much emotion is attached to the gestures and vocalizations used above. Teaching a calm, specific gesture can clarify the mental process. Children know how to tell us they don't like someone by screaming, waving their hands, or by expressing other signs of displeasure. But if your child knows how to sign or say "Don't like," this promotes language development and clarifies the specific issue calmly. The child could, alternatively, express anger or fear rather than just dislike. With language, the child might anticipate that you understand and will take care of the situation. Why teach language to children if they already know a way to communicate through screaming? Is it enough to let children scream when you could teach them to express with a sign language? Of course not. I believe dogs (and their humans) would benefit from the same opportunity for communication and mental stimulation through language development.

SIGN: NAME0–YOUR DOG'S NAME

GESTURE: As you sign, say the word *Name0.* Since my dog's name is Chal, I say *Chal* instead of *Name0.* You would say your dog's name instead.

The *human* move starts with your head facing forward. Move your head, neck, upper shoulder slowly down toward your chest, then back up. (This is not the same move as *Yes!,* which is a sharp nod down and up. *Name0* is a slower, deeper move.)

The *dog* move starts with your dog's head facing forward. The dog should move her head and neck down toward her chest, then back up.

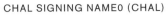
CHAL SIGNING NAME0 (CHAL)

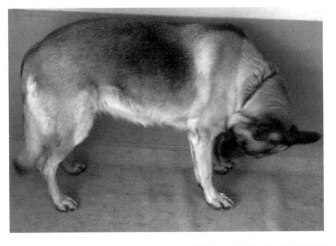

Teach the Move:

1. Entice your dog to make the move.

   - Catch your dog making the natural head move to her chest, then back to center.

   - You or an assistant place a hand or a piece of tape at her chest center.

   - With your hand or object already there, suddenly press her chest, and your dog will curl her head down and touch her chest.

2. Say/sign **_Yes! Name0_** and reward. (Her head will come back up.)

Cue the Move:

1. Entice the move and sign/say **_Sign Name0._**

2. When successful, sign/say **_Sign Name0_** and reward.

3. Repeat until you can just sign/say **_Sign Name0_** and your dog signs **_Name0,_** then reward.

Teach the Meaning:

MEANING: **_Name0_** is the dog's name.

1. Stand facing your dog, on her right side. Person2 should stand facing your dog, on her left side.

2. Point to yourself and sign/say **_IS Name1._**

3. Say/sign *Sign Name1.*

4. When your dog signs *Name1,* reward.

5. Point to Person2 and sign/say *IS Name2.*

6. Say/sign *Sign Name2.*

7. When your dog signs *Name2,* reward.

8. Point to your dog and sign/say *IS Name0.*

9. Say/sign *Sign Name0.*

10. If your dog doesn't respond, press her chest and/or place a piece of tape there.

11. When your dog signs *Name0,* reward, reward, reward.

Test the Student:

Test your dog's skill with her own name by doing the following:

1. Say/sign *Who's That?* referring to your dog.

2. When your dog signs *Name0,* sign/say *Yes! Name0* and reward profusely.

—OR—

3. Say/sign *Who's Name0?* pointing to *Name0* (your dog).

4. When your dog signs *Name0,* sign/say *Yes! Name0* and reward profusely.

Practice Exercises

Practice *Name0* in various locations, inside and outside, throughout the day.

Practice differentiating names to help your dog distinguish names by trying the following in one practice session. Before trying to differentiate, be sure your dog already solidly knows each name individually from previous lessons. Do not try to teach all names in one session.

- Say/sign *IS Name1,* referring to yourself.

- Say/sign *IS Name2,* referring to your friend.

- Say/sign *IS Name0,* referring to your dog.

- Say/sign *Who's That?* referring to Person2.

- When your dog signs *Name2,* sign/say *Yes! Name2* and reward.

Say/sign **Who's That?** referring to your dog.

- When your dog signs **Name0,** sign/say **Yes! Name0** and reward profusely.

Hold up a treat in front of Person2. Ask your dog **Who's That?** Or ask **Who's Name2?**

- When she responds by signing **Name2,** give the person half the treat, then her the rest of it.

Hold up a treat in front of yourself. Ask your dog **Who's That?** Or ask **Who's Name1?**

- When she responds by signing your name, give yourself half the treat, then her the rest of it.

Hold up a treat in front of her. Ask your dog **Who's That?** Or ask **Who's Name0?**

- When she responds by signing her name, **Name0,** give her the treat in two parts. (This should get her thinking.)

Tips

If you, your friend, or your assistant find it too complicated to both say and sign the K9Signs, just say the words.

If your dog doesn't sign **Name0,** take opportunities to say both your names often. Try taping a treat to her chest, when she tries to get it with her mouth (gesturing her name), sign/say **Name0.** If she didn't get the treat, give it to her. Don't let her eat the tape.

Comments

Teaching Chal to understand the questions **Who's That?** or **Who's Chal?** was fascinating. For many days, when I'd ask her **Who's That?** while pointing to her, she would look to her left, look to her right, and look at me, likely looking for whom I was talking about. When I'd tap her chest with a long rod, she'd tap her chest.

When I'd sign/say **Who's Chal?** while pointing to her, she would look at me and look around, seeming puzzled. Several days later when I called **Chal,** she came. I asked **Who's That Chal?** She paused, then slowly tapped her chest. She answered my question.

A fellow instructor, Ed, and I would exchange stories about dogs, (usually around the Scantron machine, the faculty "water cooler"). He told me about his Queensland heeler mix named Dusky, who played in front of a mirror from the time she was a pup. When she was about four years old, Ed would ask her, ***Where's Dusky?*** and she would run to stand in front of the mirror. Depending on how she figured this out (Ed swore he didn't teach her to do this), many interpretations could explain this behavior. But clearly Dusky showed recognition of her own name (***Name0***), reference to location (***Where***), and apparently associated a visual image (or location) in the mirror with her name. Pretty smart.

With only natural gestures, how else could a dog respond to ***Where's Dusky?*** Jump in place, on you, paw the ground, bark or look intently at you? What would a dog knowing K9Sign be able to answer? Perhaps naming herself with the sign ***Name0*** or with ***Attend.*** With developed language, a future signing dog might say ***I'm Here, In Front Of You. Can't You See Or Smell Me?***

CHAPTER 10

The Future of Signing Animals

Imagine a future with signing dogs, where they provide communicative companionship, expanded service and assistance skills, and participate in research delving into canine cognition. Companion animals who sign might clearly converse with us, reducing uncertainty and frustration for both animals and humans. Conversations would build more trust and bonding. Service dogs would relay detailed information about the environment and themselves. Veterinarians could find out why and where an animal hurts, because the patient could tell them. A dog might say she ate a sock, or that she limps due to pain in her hip, not her paw. Research might reveal that the canine brain has a true language processing center in the left hemisphere, much like ours, though less sophisticated. Technology would allow us to visualize the canine brain's blood and electrical activity during communication and thought, thereby determining the cognitive functions of specific brain areas. A shared common language such as K9Sign is a powerful tool and would enable us to expose and respect the canine cognitive processes.

Imagine the possibilities!

The AnimalSign Center's Vision

The AnimalSign vision is that nonprimate animals, such as dogs, horses, cats and others, have the opportunity to receive more than the standard training by offering them language education to become effective communicators. The AnimalSign Center, also known as Monterey Animal Language Institute, is an educational center for people and animals to learn, practice, and research methods of enhancing the ability of animals to communicate. The Center aims to enable signing animals to better communicate in their professional or home life. Professional canines might have police, search and rescue, detection (e.g., drugs, cancers, seizures, diabetes, etc.), or assistance careers. In addition to teaching and practicing signing, educators at the Center aim to study the canine capacity for true language. Currently we are focusing on AnimalSigning as the communication tool, but are also exploring additional techniques.

The AnimalSign Center's goals include affiliating with other organizations, higher educational systems, online programs, and consultants in animal and human cognition, behavior, and communication. This will facilitate research, and provide collaboration to grant professional and research degrees centering on animal literacy and language capabilities. Volunteers and interns from the community and colleges come to the Center to assist in all three aspects.

The Center will continue to train AnimalSigning instructors, who will earn AnimalSign teacher certification after coursework, training, experience, and final testing. Certification will help to maintain standardized language instruction from qualified, trained teachers. The teachers will have various contributing backgrounds, including credentials for teaching relevant subjects (e.g., bilingual, special education, deaf, hard-of-hearing, signing, and gifted students). Teachers must have high but realistic expectations, a love for communicating with animals, and solid animal academic and practical backgrounds.

The Center houses and educates its own German shepherd, Chal, and is expanding to include a Border collie (graciously offered by Dr. Karen Thompson, from TBC Border Collies, in support of AnimalSigning). The student population is now focused on dogs, horses, and cats, though other animals might be eager to be students or observers.

To embark on such a path requires tremendous support, resources, and funds. With the support and product offerings, interest of other organizations or individuals, gifts, grants, donations, and other funds, the full vision will materialize more quickly. If you are interested in being part of this vision, please contact the Center. The facility, staff, and the resources will continue to expand, enabling the language teaching, training, and research to be put to productive use, fulfilling and enhancing the lives of people and animals. Animals will use this language to enhance their own thought process and self-esteem, and extend service and companionship with us and each other.

Through the Center, many resources are available to the community to share, teach, document, and research the potential of animals to learn and use gestures in meaningful ways (as communication or as language). In addition to this book, you will find classes from AnimalSigning to those covering Communication with Manners (communication-based obedience classes). For people anywhere who want to learn, train, or teach more, the Animal-Sign Center offers the following services, products, and information:

SERVICES
- Live and Tele-Seminars
- Courses and Workshops (held at the AnimalSign Center, CSUMB Extension, AHT Programs, and TheRawConnection)
- Private and Group Tutoring
- Private Live and Phone Consultation

PRODUCTS
- *Princess! The Signing Horse: Whinny* (DVD)
- AnimalSign pamphlets

CONNECTIONS/NETWORKING

Keep in touch for information on animal communication events throughout the world. Contact me at signer@animalsign.org or follow the AnimalSign Blog at www.blogger.com/animalsigning.

Stay informed of events and the latest in signing, by visiting www.animal sign.org and signing up for:

AnimalSignNewsletter

K9SignNewsletter

EquineSignNewsletter

Signing Socials: Local gatherings for signers to exchange about their pets communications

THE GRADUATING CLASS OF 2008

From left: Lucinda and Tobee, Sandra and Fiona, Laurie and Laila, Kelly and Maya.

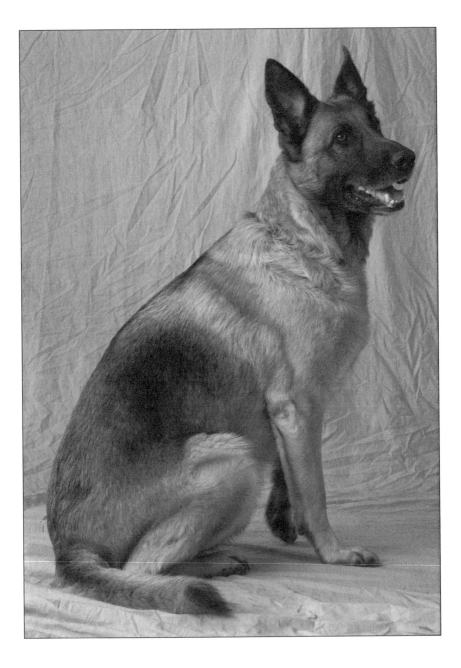

Acknowledgments

Thanks to the many animals and people who supported, each in their own way, the effort, development, and finalization of this book.

Thanks to all my supporters, students, clients, and friends, especially: to California State University at Monterey Bay Extension, the Olli program, for allowing me to share AnimalSigning Class with their Life Long Learners; to Michele Crompton for directing the program, offering the site for my classes, and for taking graduation photos; and to my students Kelly Mindham and Maya, Laurie and Laila, Sandra and Fiona, and Lucinda Andersen and Tobee (who hosted the first-ever Signing Social).

Thanks to Sharon Radel for donating her experience and skill as a veterinary technician to all my animals and for supporting AnimalSigning by inviting me to lecture to her Animal Veterinary Program classes. Thanks also go to Candice Masters, Molly Adams, and Paul Seaman for offering their friendly help with my animals as I wrote this book.

Thanks to Debbie Cruz for inviting me to explore K9Signing in both gesture and vocalization forms with her wonderful Yorkies, Taz and Anna Pepper, as well as for her friendship and care for myself and Chal. We thanked her by having Chal sign her name.

Thanks to Mary and David Liskin for helping the AnimalSign Center grow and especially for making possible the comfortable transportation of Phemie-StarLight to the AnimalSign Center when she was a puppy.

Thanks to Laura Pasten, Anne Longman, and Joni Black who offered useful and encouraging comments and exchanges on animal communication.

Thanks also to Marga Riddle for her seasoned dog-world/publishing perspective, rich experiences, wise commentary, and astute recommendations.

Thanks to May Carpenter for directing me to Eric Von Falconer, Chal's breeder. Thanks to them, the perfect "total" dog joined me on this extraordinary journey. Thanks to Harold Gale for introducing me to Dr. Karen Thompson who bred, carefully selected, and donated the Border collie puppy Phemie-StarLight. Harold also generously shared his knowledge and experiences about the socialization and cognition of Border collies (and people). His dogs have schooled him well—he is a most brilliant, diplomatic, eloquent, and compassionate human being.

Thanks to the Peninsular Women's Network in Monterey for various programs I participated in that encouraged the spotlighting of AnimalSigning and its subsequent business development. At their meetings I presented my first K9Sign showcase using stuffed animals! At their seminars I found my way to agents and the publishing industry.

Thanks to my literary agent Deirdre Mullane for guiding me through a solid proposal to a contract with Ten Speed Press. Thanks to the Random House/Crown Group for making my book available to a world-wide audience. Thanks also to my Ten Speed Press team, especially: Genoveva Llosa for her excitement about and acceptance of the proposal; my editor Veronica "Fuzzy" Randall who insured a quality production under numerous tight deadlines; talented designers Katy Brown and Colleen Cain for a beautiful and usable layout; photographer Drew Parsons for a great day of shooting with Chal; copyeditor Susan McCombs, proofreader Jean Blomquist, indexer Katherine Stimson, and production manager Mary Ann Anderson— with this team a beautiful book was sculpted.

Thanks to Diane Grindol and Misty for taking "early draft" photographs that helped me envision the final book.

Thanks to the National Writers Union, California Writers Club, and its local branch Center Coast Writers group for their many useful manuals, seminars, and networking. For astute advice and options about the literary profession, I thank Robert Pimm and Bill Minor.

Thanks to the compassionate animal scientists and the equine and canine teachers/trainers for mastering old and exploring new terrains, especially those who teach primate sign language, for making this forest trail more visible to me.

Special thanks to Dr. Francine "Penny" Patterson who visited Princess and me as I began this journey. Her useful exchanges concerning my goals and experiences with Princess, Chal, and StarLight, have been invaluable as I make signing more accessible for dogs. Penny's pioneering work with Koko the gorilla is a constant source of inspiration to me.

Very special thanks to my horse Princess who inspired me to help animals communicate better. Thanks to my dog Chal who has partnered with me to paw proof K9Sign especially for her species. Thanks to my youngster StarLight who will bring new energy to my continuing K9Sign exploration. And to all my other signing students: every move you make contributes to AnimalSign Language. Thank you.

Above all, I must acknowledge all the other animals I've had the honor to experience and learn from, starting with Snowball, Butter, Precious, Sene, Razz, Rumple, Topaz, Crystal, Tux, AngelFur, Velvet, Pastel, and my childhood neighbors at the National Zoo in Washington DC. The path Princess and I rode to signing was grounded on you.

The AnimalSigners

SEAN

Sean Senechal is the founder of AnimalSign Languages and the Animal-Sign Center in Monterey County, California. She directs the research and education at the Center, studying and developing methods to enhance the communication capabilities of animals, in particular dogs, horses, and cats. She focuses on educating her dogs Chal and Phemie, horse Princess, and cats Velvet, Pastel, and Mr. Tux. In Monterey and neighboring communities she holds seminars, workshops, and classes on AnimalSigning. Her personal, educational, and professional experiences, coupled with curiosity, intuition, and love of animals have integrated into the AnimalSign Center vision.

Her love of teaching extends to a variety of students (human, equine, canine, and feline), from those with special needs to those with special talents. She taught cell biology and physiology at University of California, Davis, and is currently an instructor at California State University at Monterey Bay (CSUMB) in the division of Social, Behavioral, and Global Studies where she teaches Human Biology and Behavior, and in the Extension Program where she teaches Canine Biology and Behavior. In the CSUMB Extension's Osher Lifelong Learning Institute, she regularly offers Canine Wellness Through AnimalSigning. At Hartnell College's Animal Health Technology Program, Sean guest lectures on behavior, communication, and signing, as well as holds workshops in Communicating with Manners (combining basic obedience with signing), for the veterinary technology resident and student dogs. At Hartnell College she teaches a biology course on Animal Language and

Learning; through E-TrainingForDogs she teaches online courses in Canine Biology, Cognition, and Communication.

Sean is a member of the Association of Pet Dog Trainers (APDT), American Behavior Society (ABS), and American Association for the Advancement of Science (AAAS).

Her diverse professional background, integrates well with teaching language to animals. She had a lengthy graduate education in biology and animal physiology, experience as a computer software programmer, quality assurance tester, manager and director, and a variety of teaching experiences in middle and high schools, colleges, and a university.

Sean obtained a bachelor's degree in sociology at University of California Berkeley, a master's degree in biology (emphasis in physiology and behavior) at California State University at San Francisco where she conducted research in exercise physiology. She also attended UC Davis graduate school in the Animal Physiology Department. There she participated in several research studies, but focused on exercise physiology, cognition and attention in humans, and academic work on learning in nonhuman primates at a UC Davis primate center laboratory. After leaving UC Davis, Senechal obtained a teaching credential from CSUMB, with a focus on science and mathematics.

A lifelong learner, her course work includes science, biology, physiology, cognition, linguistics, American Sign Language, and education courses on teaching language, science, and math to gifted, bilingual, and special education students. Observing the classrooms of teachers using sign in their deaf and hard-of-hearing classrooms she found particularly inspiring. Sean has adapted the knowledge she gained for teaching language to dogs, horses, and cats.

CHAL

The AnimalSign Center's first K9Sign student and paw proofer, Chal is a purebred German shepherd, bred and raised for the first four months by Von Falconer in Santa Cruz, California. Born in September 2003, she was a wonderful Christmas present, vivaciously coming into our home and Center. She has a sweet and friendly temperament and loves people and dogs. Though she has a high-energy working spirit, she approaches signing with a serious, thoughtful demeanor.

After adjusting to her new home, she gained obedience and some tracking skills (her natural talent). She participated in many communication experimentations and lesson plans with various approaches to K9Sign. Initially she was cautious about signing, but this evolved into eager willingness. She has endured various trials with different moves and meanings, and thus has paw-proofed signs for practical maneuvering for big dogs. Her learning milestones are transparent, making study and journaling easy. She excels at learning meaning rather than moving, probably because of her size. She enjoys inviting me to class, where she learns how to tell me what she thinks and wants.

Chal is particularly observant of Princess, my horse. Chal communicates with varying vocalizations everything Princess is doing. When Princess rolls, Chal's barks are loud, and excited. When Princess is upset or excited, Chal interprets her behavior and conveys that message to me.

PRINCESS

Princess is the first student of AnimalSign—EquineSign. She is a Dutch Warmblood/Thoroughbred mix born in spring 1993 in California. I met her in her stall at California's Stanford Barn when she was eighteen months old. The bonding was instant and inspiring. With only carrot and brush as tools, we experimented with language lessons in her stall, her on the inside and me on the outside.

When she was three, we officially became part of the same family and moved to Brandywine Ranch in Portola Valley, California. She had a huge paddock, where she could run and exercise in between signing lessons and shows. Over the years, she has mastered over one hundred tricks, many of these meaved into signs that she communicates regularly. We have invited schools and equine therapy programs to watch Princess sign. Smart, sassy, yet sensitive, Princess enjoys learning and showing off EquineSign. Princess has showcased her beauty and brains in the media, appearing on Animal Planet's *Amazing Animals* and a local television show, *Amazing Tails*.

CHAZZ

From the Stanford Barn, we brought along Chazz, a proud and stoic quarter-horse companion. Though not interested in signing, Chazz was a good horse for me to learn to ride on, in preparation for my riding Princess. Previously he had survived a California fire, though his back was scarred from burns in his saddle area. He enjoyed a peaceful life at AnimalSign Center until he died at 28.

ANGELFUR, VELVET, PASTEL, AND TUX

At Brandywine Ranch, I met AngelFur who introduced herself by lying down before me on the walking path. Later she appeared with her two kittens, Velvet and Pastel. They were born in Chazz's paddock shelter hidden in the shavings. At another ranch, I befriended Mr. Tux, a cautious but loving stray. These cats are my first feline language students.

References and Suggested Reading

Note: Because this book is focused on dogs, I've listed canine resources first. Other resources follow in alphabetical order by subject area.

CANINE COGNITION & TRAINING

Adachi, I., H. Kuwahata, and K. Fujita. (2007) "Dogs Recall Their Owners' Face Upon Hearing the Owner's Voice." *Animal Cognition.* 10 (1), pp. 17–21.

Bekoff, M., and J. Goodall. (2007). *Animals Matter: A Biologist Explains Why We Should Treat Animals with Compassion and Respect.* Boston: Shambhala Publications, Inc.

Bauman, Diane L. (2003). *Beyond Basic Dog Training.* New York: Howell Book House.

Becker, S. (2000). *Living with a Deaf Dog.* Ohio: Susan C. Becker.

Bergin, B. (2004–2005). *College Catalog,* Assistance Dog Institute.

——— (2004). *Quest.* Assistance Dog Institute. 14.

Bergin, B., and S. Hogan. (2006). *Teach Your Dog To Read.* New York: Broadway.

Burch, M., and J. Bailey. (1999). *How Dogs Learn.* New York: Howell Book House.

Canine Science Forum, July 2008, Department of Ethology, Eötvös Loránd University, Budapest, Hungary. Department of Neurobiology and Cognition Research, University of Vienna, Vienna, Austria.

Coren, S. (1995). *The Intelligence of Dogs.* New York: Bantam Books.

Donaldson, J. (1996). *The Culture Clash.* Oakland, CA: James & Kenneth Publishers.

Dunbar, Ian. (1996). *How to Teach a New Dog Old Tricks.* Oakland, CA: James & Kenneth Publishers.

———— (2004). *Before and After Getting Your Puppy.* Novato, CA: New World Library.

Fogle, B. (1992). *The Dog's Mind.* New York: Howell Book House.

Hoffman, M. (1999). *Lend Me an Ear.* Irvine, CA: Doral Publishing, Inc.

Lindsay, S. R. (2000). *Handbook of Applied Dog Behavior and Training. Vol. 1: Adaptation and Learning.* Wiley-Blackwell Publishing.

McConnell, P. (2002). *The Other End of the Leash.* New York: Ballantine Books.

Miklosi, A. (2008). *Dog Behavior, Evolution, and Cognition.* New York: Oxford University Press, Inc.

Pasten, L. (1999). *How Smart Is Your Puppy?* Tapeworm Video.

Pfaffenberger, C. (2001). *The New Knowledge of Dog Behavior.* Wenatchee, WA: Dogwise Publishing.

Pongrácz, P. (2004). "Verbal Attention Getting as a Key Factor in Social Learning Between Dog (Canis familiaris) and Human." *Journal of Comparative Psychology.* Vol. 118 (4), pp. 375-383.

Pryor, K. (2002). *Don't Shoot the Dog!* The New Art of Teaching and Training. Revised Edition. New York: Bantam Books.

Range, M., U. Aust, M. Steurer, and L. Huber, (2008). "Visual Categorization of Natural Stimuli by Domestic Dogs." *Animal Cognition* 11 (2), pp. 339–347.

Sheldrake, R. (1999). *Dogs That Know When Their Owners Are Coming Home.* New York: Three Rivers Press.

Van Kerkhove, W. (2005). "Critical Anthropomorphism vs. 'Classical' Anthropomorphism: Two Sides of the Same Coin? Not!" APDT. July/August, pp. 12–14.

CANINE LANGUAGE

Abrantes, R. (2001). *Dog Language.* Wenatchee, WA: Dogwise Publishing.

Aloff, B. (2005). *Canine Body Language: A Photographic Guide Interpreting the Native Language of the Domestic Dog.* Wenatchee, WA: Dogwise Publishing.

Bloom, P. (2004). "Can a Dog Learn a Word?" *Science* 304, pp. 1605–1606.

Burnham, D., C. Kitamura, and U. Vollmer-Conna, (2002). 'What's New, Pussycat? On Talking to Babies and Animals'. *Science* 296 (5572), p. 1435.

Coren, S. (2000). *How to Speak Dog.* New York: Free Press, Simon & Schuster.

Csanyi, V., and R. E. Quandt. (2000). *If Dogs Could Talk: Exploring the Canine Mind.* New York: North Point Press.

Fogle, B. (2006). *If Your Dog Could Talk.* New York: DK Publishing, Inc.

Kaminski, J. J. Call, and J. Fischer. (2004). "Word Learning in a Domestic Dog." *Science* 304, pp. 1682–1683.

Rugaas, T. (2005). *On Talking Terms With Dogs: Calming Signals.* Wenatchee, WA: Dogwise Publishing.

Senechal, S. (2006). *AnimalSign To You. Imagine! Signing Is Not Just for Primates Anymore.* Monterey, CA: AnimalSign & BookSurge Publishing.

———— (2008). "The Canine Sign Language: An Intellectual Stimulation" *Canis Familiaris* 1 (4) p. 24.

———— (2008). "Your Dog Signs To You," *Canis Familiaris* 1 (3) p. 26.

———— (2009). "Improve Your Communication with Animal K9Sign." *Canis Familiaris* 2 (1) p. 24.

Smith, C. S. (2004). *Rosetta Bone: The Key to Communication Between Humans and Canines.* New York: Howell Book House.

ANIMAL COGNITION

Bekoff, M., C. Allen, and G. M. Burghardt. (2002). *The Cognitive Animal: Empirical and Theoretical Perspectives on Animal Cognition.* Cambridge, MA: MIT Press.

Grandin, T., and C. Johnson. (2005). *Animals in Translation.* Fort Washington, PA: Harvest Books.

Griffin, D. R. (1976). *The Question of Animal Awareness: Evolutionary Continuity of Mental Experience.* New York: Rockefeller University Press.

———— 1984). *Animal Thinking.* Cambridge, MA: Harvard University Press

———— 1992). *Animal Minds.* Chicago: University of Chicago Press.

ANIMAL COGNITION & TRAINING

Ainslie, T., and B. Ledbetter. (1980). *The Body Language of Horses.* New York: William Morrow and Company, Inc.

Blake, H. (1990). *Talking with Horses.* North Pomfret, VT: Trafalgar Square Publishing.

Budiansky, S. (1995). *The Nature of Horses.* New York: Free Press.

Hanggi, E. B. (2001). "Can Horses Recognize Pictures?" In *Proceedings of the Third International Conference of Cognitive Science,* pp. 52–56. Beijing, China.

Lyons, J. with Sinclair Browning. (1991) *Lyons on Horses.* New York: Doubleday.

Roberts, M., and Jean Abernethy. (2002). *From My Hands to Yours.* Solvang, CA: Monty and Pat Roberts, Inc.

Senechal, S. (2003). *Princess! The Signing Horse.* (Video). Monterey, CA: AnimalSign.

BABY SIGN AND STUDIES

Acredolo, L., and S. Goodwyn. (2000). *Baby Minds: Brain Building Games Your Baby Will Love.* New York: Bantam Press.

Acredolo, L., and S. Goodwyn. (1985). "Symbolic Gesturing in Language Development." *Human Development* 28, pp. 40–49.

Garcia, J. (2004). *Sign with Your Baby.* Seattle, WA: Sign2Me Northlight Communications, Inc.

HUMAN LANGUAGE

Bloom, P. (2000). *How Children Learn the Meanings of Words.* Cambridge, MA: MIT Press.

Cairns, H. (1996). *The Acquisition of Language.* The Pro-Ed Studies in Communicative Disorders series. Austin, TX: Pro-Ed.

Chomsky, N. (2000). *New Horizons in the Study of Language and Mind.* Cambridge: Cambridge University Press.

Dunbar, R. (1996). *Grooming, Gossip and the Evolution of Language.* London: Faber and Faber.

Gardner, R. A., and B. Gardner. (1998). *The Structure of Learning. From Sign Stimuli to Sign Language.* Mahwah, NJ: Erlbaum.

Golinkoff, R. and Hirsh-Pasek, K. (1999) *How Babies Talk: The Magic and Mystery of Language Acquisition.* New York: Dutton/Penguin.

Golinkoff, R., K. Hirsh-Pasek, and D. Eyer. (2004). *Einstein Never Used Flashcards: How Our Children Really Learn—and Why They Need to Play More and Memorize Less.* Emmaus, PA: Rodale, Inc.

Horgan, J. (June 2005). "Can a Single Brain Cell Recognize Bill Clinton?" *Discover* (June) pp. 64–69.

Locke, J. L. (1993). *The Child's Path to Spoken Language.* Cambridge, MA: Harvard University Press.

McCabe, A. (1992). *Language Games to Play with Your Child.* New York and London: Insight Books.

Pinker, S. (2000). *The Language Instinct.* New York: HarperCollins Publishers.

NONHUMAN PRIMATE LANGUAGE

Fouts, R. S. and S. T. Mills. (1997). *Next of Kin.* New York: William Morrow and Co.

Goodall, J. (2000). *Jane Goodall: 40 Years at Gombe.* Washington, DC: Goodall Institute.

Gorilla, a journal published semiannually by the Gorilla Foundation, Box 620-530, Woodside, CA 94062.

Patterson, F. G. (1979). "Linguistic Capabilities of a Lowland Gorilla." Ph.D. dissertation. Stanford University (University Microfilms International Edition).

Patterson, F. G., and R. N. Cohen, (1990). "Language Acquisition by a Lowland Gorilla: Koko's First Ten Years of Vocabulary Development." *Word,* 41 (2), pp. 97–142.

Patterson, F., and E. Linden. (1981). *The Education of KoKo.* New York: Holt, Rinehart, and Winston.

Of particular interest (and inspiration) to me is Dr. Patterson's life work raising and educating Koko the gorilla. Her book *The Education of KoKo* is enlightening. Her website www.koko.org is a rich assortment and display of Koko's life, talent, and contribution. Koko has a voluminous repertoire of understood and signed words and phrases. I'm in awe of, and inspired by, their unique and rich communication and relationship.

Rumbaugh, D. M., and W. A. Hillix. (2003). *Animal Bodies, Human Minds.* New York: Kluwer/Academic Press.

Schrier, Allan M., et al. (Eds.). (1971). *Behavior of Nonhuman Primates,* Vol. 4. Academic Press.

Bird Language

Pepperberg, I. M. (2008). *Alex & Me: How a Scientist and a Parrot Uncovered a Hidden World of Animal Intelligence—and Formed a Deep Bond in the Process.* New York: HarperCollins.

Pepperberg, I. M. (2002). *The Alex Studies: Cognitive and Communicative Abilities of Grey Parrots.* Cambridge, MA: Harvard University Press.

Pepperberg, I. M., and R.J. Bright. (1990). "Talking Birds." *Birds, USA* 2 pp. 92–96.

Senechal, S. (2003). *Princess! The Signing Horse.* (DVD). Monterey, CA: AnimalSign Center.

Dolphin Language

Jerison, H. J. (1986). "The Perceptual Worlds of Dolphins. *Dolphin Cognition and Behavior: A Comparative Approach,* edited by R. J. Schusterman, J. A. Thomas, and F. G. Wood. Hillsdale, NJ: Lawrence Erlbaum.

Rumbaugh-Savage, E. S. (1993). Language Learnability in Man, Ape, and Dolphin. In *Language and Communication: Comparative Perspectives,* edited by H. Roitblat, L. M. Herman, and P. E. Nachtigall. Hillsdale, NJ: Lawrence Erlbaum.

PRIMATE SIGN LANGUAGE

Emmorey, K. (2002). *Language, Cognition, and the Brain: Insights From Sign Language Research.* Hillsdale, NJ: Lawrence Erlbaum.

LINKS

Affiliations

http://extended.csumb.edu
www.csumb.edu/olli
www.hartnell.edu/aht
www.raisingcanine.com
www.e-trainingfordogs.com
www.therawconnection.com
www.lacysbordercollies.com

Books Online

www.amazon.com
www.tenspeed.com
www.randomhouse.com
www.storey.com
www.dogwise.com

Nonprimate Animal Training & Communication

www.animalsign.org
www.assistancedog.org
www.sfspca.org
www.e-trainingfordogs.com
www.raisingcanine.com
www.apdt.com
www.cappdt.ca
www.akc.org
www.equineresearch.org
www.alexfoundation.org
www.dolphincommunicationproject.org
www.dolphin-institute.org

Primate Communication

www.koko.org
www.janegoodall.org
www.babysigns.com
www.sign2me.com
www.cwu.edu/~cwuchci
www2.gsu.edu/~wwwlrc/

Index